RAMIFICATIONS

Today's Development, Economy, Environment and Politics

A TECHNO-GANDHIAN PERSPECTIVE

DR. BALAMURALI BALAJI

RAMIFICATIONS

Today's Economy, Development, Environment and Politics

A TECHNO-GANDHIAN PERSPECTIVE

DR. BALAMURALI BALAJI

Contents

First Edition, November 2023

EBook: Amazon's Kindle Direct Publishing

Print Edition: Pothi.com, October 2023

Preamble

For more than two decades I have been pondering more about Mahatma Gandhi, his life works, methods and principles possibly because of his global admiration and inspiration by millions of people around the world. I have written four books solely based on his quotes, speeches and writings. In those books, I had paraphrased, expanded, and elucidated his ideology for the purpose of thorough understanding of not only his philosophy but to comprehend certain principles vital to our life. I had put them in my own words to help the reader discover Gandhi and his relevance more vividly in today's perspective.

With not much care about the commercial success of the book, I had selected topics and issues whichever had touched my heart causing a deep thought over in my mind. All my earlier books were an outcome of such inspiration as well as the essential dictum that everyone needs to know about Gandhi. Interestingly, I wrote "The Techno-Gandhian Philosophy", a book that speaks of modern day relevance and application of Gandhian Philosophy and gave a pragmatic approach to practice his principles in socio-political spheres. The practical, process model I suggested in that book puts Gandhi's dream into three aspects "Accountability", "Responsibility" and "Morality" – taking Gandhism towards the next step in the multitudes of complications in the technology-intense world of today. Based on this philosophy one could practice Gandhian ideals towards achieving socio-political roles and responsibilities, goals through a systematic process in steps.

Having been inclined to develop a socio-political sense for exploring the movements amongst people, communities, state and nation, I began closely observing the current affairs in my own Gandhian perspective. Even if we do not involve much in polity, some events and calamities, say pandemic, flooding, rioting etc., would force us keep a close watch on what is happening around us and in the aftermath of such disasters, as well. After all, Governance and administration, law and order, economy and commerce, society and communities, people and polity – all have a lot to observe, study and examine sparking new thoughts over the improvement and betterment of lives. I could see certain issues in a Gandhian perspective, connect them with ideals and methods Gandhi had preached in his days. Such an association of present day problems with his dictum often led to finding unique ways to generate solutions and resolve conflicts. Finding relevance of Gandhi in conflict-ridden societies and violent communities would surely give us a proposition in the process of resolving issues.

"Ramifications" is not only a commentary on various issues that are plaguing today's world, especially India, but a potpourri of my Gandhian thoughts, suggestions and, to some extent, criticisms as well. Today's Economy, Development, Environment and Politics was not like years ago. Atleast about two decades before things have changed in the world rapidly in the post-globalization era, so rapidly enough to bring people much closer than ever shrinking the world within reach. Computers and communications have changed our lives to ease out our work, no doubt. At the same time, it has challenged our lives so heavily to pay a price in terms of degrading our innate values and sustainable living. From exploring the Moon to Mars, rockets to drones, robots to artificial intelligence, developments have leaped into a new high; alas, ordinary things are still hanging in loose with no ways to tighten the screws.

Satyagraha, fasting protests, ashram life, Sarvodaya, and constructive programmes – are all still seen as a mysterious package of techniques and means for attempting to resolve the crisis prevailing in the socio-political planes. With the world fast moving towards modernity and technologies, Gandhi is very often mistaken and his principles misinterpreted. His Ahimsa is as questionable as it was in the beginning during his times. Today's youth could not find answers for matters like Ahimsa and Satyagraha being a possible solution for their ends. Making them realize how humanitarian work, love and passion is much more powerful than science and technology is a wearisome judgment.

It is important to understand the ideological Gandhi, the causes and effects of his words that have worked during his freedom movement. It is also significant to find a relevance and applicability of those words in the current scenarios which necessitate a deep analysis and study of his life and history. Today, we see experts and leaders claiming that a problem could be solved by Gandhian means. Some others, we see that following the path of Gandhi would suffice to weaken the evil forces threatening the world. Sadly, no one could reckon the exact methodology or model to practice to meet the key results. Nevertheless, the world has been governed and run by his principles and tenets in order to uphold social justice, moral values and peace.

The book "RAMIFICATIONS: Today's Economy, Development, Environment and Politics" is a collection of essays portraying the corollaries of certain key issues that shook the world these days. Whereas my earlier books explored how Gandhi's principles influenced and inspired people on personal transformation, 'RAMIFICATIONS' is intended to seek a relevance of

Gandhian existence in today's developmental, economic, environmental and political aspects.

The objective is to promote Gandhian values and highlight its relevance and prevalence in all aspects of today's world. The book delves into various issues of today's politic and society, by taking news and events for discussion, genuinely advocating Gandhian connotations and its relevance. Needless to mention that I have put my criticism as and when required while emphasizing a particular point that goes against any known law or logic.

This edition of the book includes topics such as "Bridging Gandhi and present-day politics", "Conceptualizing Sarvodaya in today's context", "Localized Economy", "Gandhian deliberation towards solving International Conflicts", "Developmental impact on environment", "Covid-19", "Pricing and Inflation", "Russia-Ukraine War" and "Climate Change: Issues and Actions". All these issues portray the appalling revelations of Gandhism in modern day's context and the importance of Gandhian approach not only for reconciliation but to grasp a clear understanding of the issues. The topic on the pandemic "Covid-19" is included in this book so as to find a comparative relevance of Gandhian way of lifestyle and living with the restrictions and limited resources during the pandemic days.

The topic, "Bridging Gandhi and present-day politics" appraises political ideology and political agenda in India's post independent politics. It also discloses focuses on the political situation in North-East India. "Conceptualizing Sarvodaya in today's context" is a political perspective and scope for Sarvodaya to bring changes in the ways we work day-to-day. "Gandhian deliberation towards solving International Conflicts" discusses the trivial U.S. relationship with the North-Korean peninsula and nuclear Iran. "Localized Economy" compares the Gandhian dictum of economy with that of current days' economic development. The topic "Developmental impact on environment" concerns the environmental damages caused due to massive industrialization these days and discusses how the government's Environmental Impact Assessment and National Green Tribunal addresses the issues related to it. "Covid-19" does a comparative study on simpler ways of life in a pandemic-changed world with the Gandhian lifestyle while purveying the same with a scientific point of view. It also includes a commentary on "Pricing and Inflation" analyzing the cause of economic recession and its effects on the market price. The section 'Russia-Ukraine War' is all about the woes of the world due to war as it tries to throw light on humanity, hope and peace elucidating ways to restore them. "Climate change: Issues and Actions" briefs worldwide impacts due to adverse changes in climatic conditions and what the solutions on shelf to combat it.

I hope the readers would find this book very useful in recalling the key affairs of the world and getting a deeper understanding of why and how such things happen. To simply put it, readers will get a broad, pragmatic idea behind today's economy, development, environment and politics.

In completing this work amid various work and hindrances, I would acknowledge my sincere thanks to my family for showing passion and love besides caring during the time spent on this book.

-    Dr. Balamurali Balaji

Bridging Gandhi and present-day politics

Politics in India is more dynamic and vibrant than that of in other countries as she was born in the world as a sovereign state in a peculiar and astounding way as envisioned and guided by Mahatma Gandhi. In the post-independent India, politics has taken various twists and turns headed by various governments formed by different parties and leadership. The political path of India has witnessed various parties and factions, coalitions and calculations that aimed at forming a government at the centre. However, the Indian National Congress and Bharatiya Janata Party – are the two parties rivaling each other based on ideological differences and political legacy they claim to possess. The Congress governments headed by Gandhiji's prominent aide Jawaharlal Nehru for the first two decades and other governments led by his successors have a lot to tell about politics and ideological approaches towards various issues in the nation. Similarly, the emergence of the Bharatiya Janata Party during the late 90s in the last century with its Hindutva ideology has greater implications on the whole of the political scene and policies that govern India.

Here I am trying to define political ideology from an empirical point of view exploring its scope, individualistic character, and its transformational, divisive and reflective nature. It also points out the ideology behind contemporary politics with reference to that of Gandhian economics. The state of Gandhian ideology in current day's politics is also discussed with the context of political parties taking up their political agenda as against their ideologies.

What Gandhi is for today's youth and for today's politicians, Why Gandhi's principles need to be taught, thought and trailed by modern political thinkers and leaders, and how his ideology works in the main-stream politics along with the north-east India policy – these are all certain questions I ought to address here.

Overview

"*I want world sympathy in this battle of right against might*" – When Mahatma Gandhi affirmed these words while marching from his ashram to the coastal town of Dandi in Gujarat to defy the British government's salt tax, his ideology of Satyagraha, the truth force was invoked as against the ruling and the atrocities of the imperial empire not just in India but all around the world. His adherence to Ahimsa and Truth, as he used to refer them as two lungs without which he could not have breathed in his life, shaped up into a new political movement for India's freedom struggle. His nonviolent fasting and protests in apartheid South Africa which thus far felt as poor, indentured workers' picketing and labours' movement, was unanimously hailed as a 'large scale transformation' of the man called Mohandas Gandhi and also the much reclusive, impoverished nation called India.

One man's ideology has transformed a country into a nation, freeing her from enslavement, and setting a new democratic ideology what the rest of the world can see as a political path towards resolving conflicts. Embracing of such a peaceful, nonviolent ideology by leaders like Jawaharlal Nehru, Sardar Vallabhbai Patel, Abul Kalam Azad, Sarojini Naidu, Rajendra Prasad and many others was just a reflection of ideology in work.

When Jawaharlal assumed his Prime Minister ship in 15th of August, 1947, on the day of India's Independence, only a few had believed that ideology of truth and justice through nonviolent means would survive so eternally, century after century. Yet, adversaries and fundamentalists have got their own stick which gave jolts in the form of regional partitions and separations adding more vibrancy and liberty to aspirants who wanted to freely articulate their ideologies and goals.

Nature of political ideology

Political ideologies are periodical; they change from years to years as with the people's needs and nation's wants. The world has seen many leaders who have changed their ideology and perspective when it comes to a state where they had to shed their persistence on issues and plans that shape up their nations. Only very few ideologies have lasted for centuries due to its much wider scope and their substantial execution of theory into practice on perennial issues what the humanity is facing all the times. While many of his followers like Nehru, Patel, Rajaji detached themselves from their quest to end Jinnah's plan of creating new nation for Muslims, Gandhi held his vision of unified India to which he held all his breathe until his death. Even after independence, his teachings stand as moral pillars enduring the crisis paving the ways for peace and harmony in the political stage. His one nation theory is construed as 'Akanda Bharat' (Extended India) by right wing politicians.

Political ideologies are individualized; it was a set of guidelines and doctrines for a collective force to work in unison to counteract a problem or crisis what the people are facing collectively as a group or society or nation. Nevertheless ideologies are propounded and molded by people who distinctively take their principles to the core of the issues they dealt with. Great men are symbolized by their ideologies. Mahatma Gandhi, Karl Marx, Abraham Lincoln are just a few individuals who effectively preached their approach, principles and methods in resolving conflicts for their people.

Political ideologies are transformational; once practiced by followers, ideologies tend to transform people to any extent. It is the strength and mass support an ideology receives from the people determines the life of an ideology. Communism and Socialism cease to exist widely not because of changing economic conditions but also due to the incursion of capitalist markets and varied democratic methods. Once the followers of Karl Marx, Cuba's Fidel Castro emerged as revolutionist leader of his homeland taking it on to the path of dignified progress. The main accomplice of Gandhi, Jawaharlal Nehru led post-independent India for more than two decades. Gandhi's followers elsewhere in the world viz. Martin Luther King Junior II, Nelson Mandela, Aung Suyu Ki, Desmon Tutu and the Dalai Lama have become transformational icons changing the lives and the nations setting a new dogma of service to humanity.

Political ideologies are divisible; they are represented in the form of political parties, movements and factions. Gandhi's political methods and principles are adopted lately by smaller parties and groups. In South India, Dravidian political ideology as propounded by Periyar EV Ramasami and CN Anna Durai has seen many divisions with newer parties branching out of evolving principles as against the original ideology. Indian National Congress started by Alan Octavian Hume in 1885 has also undergone various divisions and factions over the last century reason being the regional interests, quest for the seat of power and not to mention the vote bank politics which is becoming popular and widespread during last twenty years. The essence of all such divisions and branching out is nothing but the complexity in following the original dictum even during the changing political conditions and interests of the leaders who keep their focus on their seat of power and to some extent for the development and progress of the country.

Political ideologies are reflective; Even though an ideology is designed and preached by individuals and distinctive leadership by them, more often it reflects the people's cultural, ethical and religious sentiments. When Muslims in India was driven by a desire of a separate nation for them, it was the religious divide that stood first to form the Muslim League but not the freedom struggle in front of them. The Hindu dominant struggle was in a way intercepted by Muslim interests and exquisite leadership by Mohammed Ali Jinnah shaped the ideology of League. The transition of the Hindu Maha Sabha that was blamed for the murder of Mahatma Gandhi into Rashtriya Swayam Sevak Sangh and later on to Jan Sangh and more recently to Bharathiya Janata Party is a perfect example for how ideologies are determined by cultural facets and religious beliefs. Not many outfits representing the cultural and religious outlooks in the country had had a distinguished leader of their own for many decades. The success and failure of the ideology is as much important as the leadership itself. When people reflect ideologies, it becomes transformational whereas while the ideologies shaping up over the course of changing times and people's beliefs, it becomes transitional.

Contemporary views on Gandhian ideology
Gandhian economics is one area from which we derive a plenty of lessons and approaches towards solving today's

problems. While no government has been so 'swadeshi' as preached by Mahatma Gandhi, certain principles have been consistently put into practice in the form of various schemes such as decentralization, rural economy, and education as a tool for self-development, production by the masses and indigenous productions. Between 'sovereignty' and 'swadeshi', governments are swinging from one end to another trying to balance both progress and moral progress. Most of these schemes are being aided by foreign investments and being implemented through technologies and methods practiced by developed nations in the world. The lust of the schemes is lost therefore due to the foreign elements and moral factor as perceived by Gandhi also gets eroded. Indigenous outlook is totally missing as our thoughts continue to rove around western ideologies and models.

India has been popularly called as the "dump-yard of the west" because of the increasing wants of the people, corporate, business houses, needless to mention, the state and central governments. If it is not for cultural migration as feared by some, it would definitely mean for the globalization and liberalization policies. Nowadays, people started believing that these two are the only 'buzz' words for our own survival. We started walking along with the other developed countries in order to create new economies and venues for trade and commerce without knowing limits of our own needs.

Ideologically, our politicians are not too far from that of Gandhi's and not too closer either. Gandhian methods such as fasting, picketing, and other nonviolent ways of protesting to seek social justice and to meet political ends – are all seen as basic requisites for being a politician, to whichever ideology he follow or to whatever party he belongs to. To that extent, Gandhi's ideology has pioneered the elements of democracy. What Gandhi had dreamt of India in terms of governance and public service is still a dream and is not entirely achieved by any. What Gandhi stood for in terms of character and ethics has vanished completely from public life.

Many people believe that Gandhian economics was just an outcome of his spiritual and moral values which won't be fitting in today's modern and micro economics. His language of economics was too simple and in lower order as that today's' economists would not have understood and absorbed it essentially for today's economic needs. Khadi, Spinning, Handicrafts were soul and substance of his ideology to carry out his political maneuvers. Today's political agenda or manifesto of any party would surely read different when it is compared to that of Gandhi's. Modernization of transports viz., rail service, buses and air planes, creation of new airports, technology parks, wireless stations, high-tech roads, importing of goods and services, digital and e-governance are just a few items to mention how our national agenda has turned so technical in order to match with the so called 'world standards'. Gandhi has clearly stated, *"This again seems impossible without great nations ceasing to believe in soul-destroying competition and to multiply wants and increasing their material possessions. Multiplicity of wants has no fascination for me. They deaden the inner life in us.......A certain degree of physical harmony and comfort is necessary, but above a certain level it becomes a hindrance instead of a help."*

Dominant by corruption, lavish life-style, publicity, misuse of power and hypocrisy, today's politicians lack true character and substance of what Gandhi and his contemporaries possessed during those years. Icons representing today's ideologies are mediocre ways for wooing people on to their sides. Every party and ideology proclaims to work for maintaining decency and cleanliness in performing their political duties.

Unfortunately, we see them all just in their talks and manifesto or in the news.

The most popular belief among the people is that a person of good nature and character like that of one following Gandhian ideals is not welcomed in political arena. With all the chaos and sleaze games becoming standards, people tend to omit persons who stuck firmly to his ideology. *"Politics without principles"* – one of the seven sins Gandhi stated has become a mantra for achieving political gains. Principled men are sidelined and put up in struggle to perform his bit of public service. Politics without ethics and principles must be banned in first place to clean up the entire political stage. While all the parties are pledging to work for the downtrodden and the deprived, parties based on caste, religion and sects are increasingly polluting the political atmosphere. Contrarily, smaller parties cropping up on a day-to-day basis making tall claims on practicing Gandhian principles are nothing but mockery and deception.

Political agenda or ideology?

The conflict between the upper caste Hindus and untouchables was another tenuous issue that hauled the compromising efforts from Gandhi. His fast-unto-deaths have put both the factions into a state of hollowness, but diluting the whole conflict, bringing harmony. The same Harijan cause has become a burning issue stunning the country even after independence as the low-caste Hindus wanting for amendments in the reservation of Schedule Castes/Scheduled Tribes in the areas of education, jobs and welfare schemes announced by the government and public sector. 50% of SC/ST reservation implemented by the VP Singh government as per the recommendations from the Mandal Commission in 1991 was an outcome of series of riots and violence meted out in the capital city of New Delhi. Secular parties favouring the reservation bill were silently watching the insurrection carried out by the right wing fundamentalists and anti-reservationists. Assuming the welfare of Harijans is the right cause even today after Gandhi's endeavors, it was not achieved as dreamed by Gandhi. The Parliamentary powers are keen on carrying out the tasks laid out in front of the nation by the Father of the Nation, but not perfectly along the path of nonviolence and truth.

Similarly Women's reservation bill passed in 2010 by the Vajpayee government was aimed at empowering women in order to place them at par with men folks in all walks of life including the quota for electing women in all administrative and legislative bodies had sent some turbulence by the opposition parties. The bill got passed in the Rajya Sabha, but not in Lok Sabha.

As Gandhi said, *"A woman's intuition has often proved truer than man's arrogant assumption of superior knowledge"*, women's contribution to the development and welfare of the country is remarkable enough that man had experienced it during the freedom struggle as well as in serving the nation later. So what is notable here is that the nation is so particular about castes and creeds and gender equality is a must for humanity.

Hindu-Muslim unity is one of the key issues mongering for centuries ever since Mughals began ruling the parts of the country from 14th century. It turned into a stand-off during the India's independence movement for which Gandhi had dedicated his truest heart and soul until the end. His nonviolent means seeking for an amicable settlement over the divided nation between Hindus and Muslims might not have witnessed a positive end, but had left an unending scar on the secular nature and religious harmony of the nation. Pakistan, carved out of India with disputed land of Kashmir has been a persistent conflict-prone region generating fight after fight between the armies of the two nations leaving bloodshed and casualties even into the interior parts of the state of Jammu and Kashmir, fueled by terror attacks and militant insurgencies. Besides Kashmir, India and Pakistan, having fought two wars in 1969 and 1973, has been calling out their supremacy of power each other very often making peace a big challenge in the region.

Another challenging phase in the Indian politics that disrupted Hindu-Muslim unity in a scary way was during the regime of PV Narsasimha Rao. On 6th December 1992, Babri Masjid in Ayodhya in the state of Uttar Pradesh was demolished by Hindu Kar Sevaks headed by organizations viz, Vishwa Hindu Parishad, Bajrang Dal and RSS allegedly provoked by the BJP senior leader LK Advani. Hindu organizations claimed that the Masjid was built by destroying a Ram temple that was revered as Ram Janma Bhoomi during the Mughal Raj. Followed by Masjid demolition in 1996, violence and unrest reigned in many parts of northern India killing around 2000 people. What happened then to Gandhi's ideology and so-called Gandhian spirit held by the centre and the state governments? What made the myth and religious fanaticism taking over the historical monument into dust? Secularism, religious harmony and all promises made by political parties and leaders was demolished in few hours. It was neither the Congress's violation nor the state BJP's fault at crushing the religious beliefs of a minority group, it was believed. But, then at the end of the trial, justice prevailed amid gloominess as LK Advani, Murli Manohar Joshi, a and Vinay Katiyar were charged with criminal conspiracy by the top court in 2017.

What is disguised in the event of demolition of Babri Masjid is that the overriding of one ideology of "Hindutva" over all other ideologies that speak of secular, neutral and pervasive approach towards religious conflicts. Building of Ram Mandir might be a political agenda of BJP but it could not be executed during the Congress regime at the centre. The Hindu ideological uproar that went into skirmish beating all existing ethical, moral laws was nothing but an outburst of ideological clash over power and supremacy. The covetous minds behind Babri Masjid case were not just limited to Hindu uproar. On 8th August, 2017, the Uttar Pradesh Shia Central Waqf Board, holding the one-third of the disputed site as ordered by the court verdict, indicated that their Sunni counterpart was not interested any amicable settlement with the Hindus.

Political agenda or ideology, either of them is possible with peaceful, passive approach. Unfortunately, violent ideas and action plans was not successful in its entirety. *Ram Mandir* is still a dream and is becoming BJP's trump card in its election manifesto. Had Gandhi was alive in the midst of such a crisis, he would have built a *mandir* next to mosque and would have called for nonviolent resolution, guiding the Hindu groups to go in accord with Muslim leaders based on talks and negotiation.

Gandhi and youth

Gandhi was firm on the need for spiritual training for students besides being trained them intellectually and physically. *"The spiritual training,"* according to him, *"is the training of the spirit itself; to develop the spirit is to build character and to enable one to work towards knowledge of God and self-realization."* The young minds should be properly trained to know about themselves, their culture and religion. Training the spirit of youth is possible through the character and living style of their teachers, who may be held as role models in those little minds. Gandhiji worked as a teacher in Tolstoy farm in 1911-12 and during his tenure, he imposed himself an increased discipline and restraint to be a role model for the youngsters living with him.

A student with the disturbed mind cannot produce desired results. Needless to say what would happen to the people surrounding him? Just like a single rotten apple spoils the whole basket of fruits, an agitated student would set a wrong example for the whole student's community. And, there needs a pacifying act or support from the teachers or elders to spiritualize and tranquil his mind to maintain a healthy environment.

Spirituality is to practice, not to learn or preach. The spiritual teacher should emphasize how to practice it rather than just teaching what and why it is done. One of the salient aspects of spirituality is meditation. A student should be taught first to do this for few minutes every day. It could be combined with the prayer, individually or collectively. A few minutes of meditation would help students to refresh their minds and enable free thinking. Meditation along with prayers would clean up the blockades in their heads that worked all day along.

Today's students are more of practitioners than of listeners. Once they got to know something, they try to redo or imitate the same. Elders and teachers must live as role models so as to inspire the younger generation to follow. Gandhi's ideals of non-violence, truth, justice and peace need to be understood from a student's point of view. They can't be taught or fed into today's youth unless we have a firm belief and a way of life following those ideals.

Politics is all about serving the nation and for welfare of the people. Every issue must be dealt with nonviolently. Students and youth shall have to have a keen outlook in following a political ideology in a nonviolent manner. Political parties, despite all the differences with the Gandhian ideology, have to understand the essence of Gandhi's life messages in order to attain their goals and wishes. Democracy is susceptible to violence if not handled properly. Today's youth who indulges in democratic methods of protesting for their rights and for the wants of the society shall have to keep restraint. Gandhi's principles of celibacy (*Brahmacharya*), control of palette, truth, ahimsa, bread labour, fearlessness have greater messages for today's youth to follow.

North-East India

Mahatma Gandhi and his ideology had had a greater inspiration and impact in the land of North-East India even during the freedom struggle movement. Inspired by Mahatma Gandhi, Trilochan Pokhrel of Sikkim, the first sikkimese freedom fighter of Gorkha origin, propagated Swadeshi among the peasants in the region, changed his attire to cotton Dhoti and wooden slippers. Rani Gaidinliu of Nagaland was a spiritual and political leader who worked tirelessly for the upliftment of people and secularism spent decades of her life in imprisonment by the British rulers. Kushal Konwar of Assam, a strict follower of Gandhian principles and believer of non-violence lived the ideal life of austerity and peace. He is still memorable as a hero of the north-east for protesting the British and hanged during the Quit India Movement.

In the post-independent India, the North-East policy as framed by the Nehru government had initiated various development projects in agriculture, education, health, food and industries. However, militancy and insurgency along the eastern borders have taken development initiatives aback as they continue to pose challenge to peace and harmony in the region.

Rajiv Gandhi had won remarkable peace deals in the North-East region with Mizo peace accord that brought the Mizo National Front guerillas to the democratic process and electing its leader Pu Laldenga to replace a Congress leader as the Chief Minister of the state. During his regime, six-year long Assam agitation against infiltrators ended with the emergence of Bodo movement gaining ground to bring a peaceful settlement in the region.

Few changes made in India's North-East policy by A.B. Vajpayee during the early years of this century are seen as breakthrough initiatives that could bring stability in the region. Instituting several autonomous councils, setting up of separate ministry for development of North-East region, divestment of 10% from each ministry to the region and other initiatives such as Bodo peace accord have put the concern of the North-East in the mainstream national agenda.

With these changes happening at the political arena in the form of policy and political agenda, North-East region might have to unify among themselves with an ideology, nonviolent and peaceful along the lines of Gandhian model of development, in order to face challenges posing in future. Such an ideology shall cater to the localized needs of the north-eastern states. It would bring more strength and power to the natives. It would embrace the newer avenues opening at the global front and also guard their native values. Even the policy of "think globally, act locally" won't be suffice for the North-East as the centre-state relationship has become saturated with the prolonged execution of the past and presently announced policies. Talks and communication with the centre regarding the border issues and separatism are not suffice as they are modeless and or otherwise do exist with weak bases. Nativity and cultural diversity shall be understood within the framework of the centre's North-East policy with the arising of the Gandhian ideology that gives a fitting answer to the problems. Gandhian ideology and model of development would keep the North-East at the onus of the country as a whole. To compete in the complex political situations caused by nationalist forces at the one end and the separatist forces at the other end, the North-East shall "think locally, act locally" to obtain a strategic win. Its innate and indigenous options would come on hand-in-hand to support such an ideology.

Being the representation of minority in numbers, (out of 543 seats in Lok Sabha, 8 states of North East region contribute only 25), the North-East region shall have to look on to the issues such as religious divide, caste based politics, narrow vision of politicians and social degradation within the states so as to ensure that they make their policy clear and stand-perfect. Moreover, the issues like AFSPA in Manipur, Sikkim and Nizoram must be dealt on an as-is-where-is basis, but not as a never-ending battle of the people. Constructive work, development projects and welfare schemes shall be given due importance rather than submitting themselves to the petty political games and faulty assurances by the political parties. People of the North-East must strive to keep such positive stride towards resolving the issues arising within. Demands like minority appeasement and autonomy of district and state level administration need more nonviolent, constructive approach with a Swadeshi touch. Production by the masses, local economy and *sarvodaya* units must be built in accordance with the needs of the state.

Summary

Political ideologies are far too varying in the North-East region. Ideologies work for their own existence. They are for propagating the issues only and are hypothetical. No single ideology would solve all the problems of the day. Nonetheless, the North-East India needs a unified, nonviolent, peaceful, decentralized, indigenous ideology that would work for the betterment of the people. Such an ideology shall have to provide means at the socio-economic-political levels to see an overall development. Parties coming to power have their own agenda. People of the North-East shall choose the right ideology for staying in the race for power and prosperity; shall opt for the right agenda to carry out for their welfare and development. With its own nativity and cultural background, identifying its preferences for development is a challenging task. Students' union and women empowerment in the past have achieved to some extent towards this end. Newly formed groups and parties shall re-organize, re-think and re-formulate their goals and objectives along the Gandhian model of development.

Amid all the insurgencies along the borders and upsurges within the states, one has to strive for inner peace. Individual peace is the outcome of Gandhian ideology. Collective peace must be attained along the same path as well.

Conceptualizing Sarvodaya in today's context

Mahatma Gandhi translated the work of Ruskin's "Unto the Last" in Gujarati with the title "Sarvodaya" meaning "Welfare of all". Ever since he started the Sarvoday Sangh, constructive work and economic activities in the country have been geared up to a new level.

It conceptualizes how Sarvodaya provides means to exercise economic equality in society and governance in today's context. It also explores certain schemes like demonetization, prohibition, rural-agro industrialization and India against corruption movement with a Sarvodayan point of view. More importantly, I discuss the basis and need for Gandhian Sarvodaya in the bewildered world of today's political philosophies like Socialism and Communism.

Overview

Sarvodaya, one of the salient ideas of Mahatma Gandhi during the days of freedom struggle movement has put the people of the nation at the lowest stratus into the onus of not just the freedom movement, but also into the realms of constructive development and village economy. How

Gandhi used Sarvodaya from his Sevagram Ashram was a history. Anasakthi is the basis for his sarvodaya movement which brought millions of people together and made them think about self-development and home-economy. Antodaya came as an outcome from Sarvodaya. The mantra *"Rise of all"* evoked the rise of individuals.

His successors pulled this mantra, Vinobaji in particular, into their conceptualization of Sarvodaya in the post-independent India. Vinoba's Bhoodan, Gram Dan and other constructive works took this mantra to the rise of every individual, to the bottom-most of the country and to the greater extent of equality among the people. Freedom is the right from one's birth whereas owning a land is the right to live. Landless poor could not taste freedom without peaceful living. Sarvodaya purified millions of land owners and Zamindars who owned surplus land; it gave them opportunity to purify their hearts by the means of Dan and Dharma.

Sarvodaya and public participation

"Sarvodaya says that if a principle is accepted by a majority and is still being disregarded, then it is a fit case for Satyagraha; but if a principle is accepted by us but

not by the majority, then it is a matter for education and not for a. The principle that there should be no individual ownership of land is not accepted by the majority only we believe in it, and therefore it is a matter of education, and not of Satyagraha."

Therefore, Sarvodaya leads to the welfare from lowliest of the lowest to welfare of all by all means. It comprises both the right hood and learning. The constructive aspect of Sarvodaya has been implemented in the form of Sarvoday sanghs and forums all over the country to pull the deprived and the needy to build their own economy. Spinning, handlooms, Khadi, education, handicrafts and all man-made, hand-made products emerge as local economy feeding the numerous villages across the nation.

When the welfare of the people is disregarded as in the case of prohibition in Tamilnadu, Satyagraha must be the righteous choice for closing the liquor shops. Social activists like Sasi Perumal were trying to explicate this idea into practice. Large number of people gathered for his pleading to the state government for a liquor policy to control the use of liquor by millions of innocent people. Despite the support of the people for his month-long Satyagraha the state has witnessed only violent means and rebellious ways. The definite meaning of Sarvodaya, *'rise of all'* and the *'welfare of all'*, has been completely sidelined in this issue as the state witnessed a serious law and order problem for a while. A proper, nonviolent way of protest or another Satyagraha to bring liquor policy is still due in the state.

On 8th November, 2016 Indian economy has took a sudden twist that banned rupee notes of higher denominations. The Prime Minister's announcement of banning the ₹500 and ₹1000 notes came as a 'remedy' for controlling black money market. People returned all their money in the banks. People suffered and waited in long queues in front of the ATMs to get the restricted amount of cash set by the Reserve Bank of India. People believed that the measure is for the welfare of all; to stop the rich to plunder the poor; to clean-up the economy. People bore all the sufferings for months to recover from the ill-effects of the ban. Despite the silent suffering resulted into a peaceful solution after many hardships, as a whole the economy could not be restored back. Sarvodaya has been implemented not in the right spirit. The fundamental aspects of Truth and Justice from the institutional part of the society have failed the fullest ethics of Sarvodaya. Instead of putting the whole nation in to this mayhem, black money launderers must have been identified and brought to justice. The scheme with the right motive must follow the path of Sarvodaya. Majority of people believe that a different way of dealing with black money launderers could have done justice to Sarvodaya.

"In the happiness of the subjects lays his happiness, in their welfare his welfare. Whatever pleases himself he shall not consider as good, but whatever pleases his subjects he shall consider as good."

Sarvodaya and economic development

Farming and agriculture has long been seen as the backbone of India's economy. India has vast, rich land for cultivation as farmers and peasants continually growing the food grains and cereals which constitute the main palate of every citizen. Methods of farming used in the country have a long tradition and the credit must be borne to the community of our ancient farmers who take them generation after generation. For the same reason, agriculture was once popularly hailed as *"God's profession"*. Today's farming is not that divine. It exerts pressure, greediness, economic rivalry, monetary losses and even slavery. More number of farmers are running out of this profession due to expansion of cities, industrial development, and depletion of resources leading them deprived of their right to call them as the "sons of soil". Lands once owned by landlords and zamindars have been divided into pieces with each piece owned by individual farmers. One must recall the "Boodhan" movement of Vinoba which first initiated the transfer of ownership of lands to the landless. Agriculture, even though given priority by every government, farmers are not happy these days. They live in despair as they were neglected in the past. The main reason for this feeble condition is that the increase of natural disasters. Due to change in climatic conditions, unexpected rainfalls, flooding, storms and cyclones are on the rise causing irrecoverable damage. Besides, farming affected by artificial factors such as blockades in distribution channels and pricing conflicts.

Governments are not doing enough to tackle the problems created artificially and those arise from nature. Monetary compensations to meet the failures have made the farmers lazier than ever turning agriculture into an unwanted profession. Market conditions are also not so good enough to see the marginal profits. Fluctuations in conditions for transportation, buying prices and volume of production cause serious problem in building an agro-economy of its own. Channels of marketing the products from village groups and Sarvodaya groups must be augmented to promote local agro-economy.

For years, Sarvodaya has been the fundamental aspect of what we call rural industrialization. The growth of Silk industry, food processing, cosmetic items, paper, matches and oil, textiles, organic farming, dairy products and all other forms of today's agro industries must be attributed to the social groups and cluster of village people who had once actively involved in promoting their village economy. Sarvodaya activities contribute to meet the survival needs and rare needs of the society with the use of Self-Help groups and other user groups in the rural areas. Small-sized Sarvodayan community has today grown into a much developed Rural Economic Zone with the required tools and technologies adhering to the strict man-machine equitable policy. Self-reliant villages have become a possibility these days.

Gandhiji dreamt, *"Working for economic equality means abolishing the eternal conflict between labour and capital"*. Sarvodaya stands as a non-violent system of government for realizing this dream. *"A society or nation constructed non-violently must be able to withstand attack upon its structure from without or within"* he said. Sarvodaya teaches us this great message of Swaraj. We will no longer be restricted by the limitations set by the west or machines imported from elsewhere.

John Ruskin in his *"Unto the Last"* wrote, 'Political *economy is no science at all. We see how helpless it is when labourers go on a strike. The masters take one view of the matter, the operatives another; and no political economy can set them at one."* Labour and Capital has a continued conflict that never ceases to exist. Sarvodaya is also not a science. It is not a method either. Yet, it could be the best possible solution to draw a line between these two monstrous powers. The systemic organization of people for the purpose of a common cause yielding a common welfare will be a universal phenomenon for construction from the bottom most layer of the society. A sort of communal unity has to be attained to walk along the path of Sarvodaya to achieve such goals. It does not mean political unity which may be imposed. It requires a tremendous amount of truth, love and just for bringing unity among the people- ignorant and innocent.

The pace of economic development in today's world is unpredictable and immeasurable. The dynamics of economic development is not well understood by citizens in terms of statistical numbers as presented by the governments. While the mercantile economy accumulates wealth in the hands of the riches, competitive economy has widened the gap between the rich and the poorer.[4] People will not be happy in both these economies as they have to remain neglected or underbid one another. Sarvodaya system of governance can ensure economic equity just as the government fixes wages and salaries according to the gradation of posts. And, that will be the true economics for the welfare of all; economics of justice. It would place the people on track as they learn to do justice and be righteous and to work for moralistic, constructive development.

Sarvodaya and political philosophies

J.C. Kumarappa has rightly put the difference between Socialism, Communism and Gandhian economy in terms of Sarvodaya. *"Socialism and Communism think of the nation as one unit, India's trade is not one unit. When we talk in terms of Indian trade or Indian wealth, we are not referring to homogeneous things. We are concerned with individuals and not India as a whole. Our outlook must be universal."* Somehow, India cannot be construed as a fully socialistic nation for it has to deal with diverse range of individuals comprising various culture, religion, language and customs. Whereas the Communism bother about the material welfare and possession of wealth by the state, Gandhian connotation of the state meets the spiritual, moral and economic development of every single human being living in the state. And that was the message Gandhi transmitted across the country through his ashrams and constructive programmes. Even as the freedom struggle movement was at its high, he never failed to check with the local economic development that spun around spinning and charkha. If every individual comes to understand self-reliance and self-sufficiency, the whole nation could walk towards self-government and economic freedom. Accordingly, Sarvodaya becomes a system of implementation for many years even after independence at the local level and further scaled up to any level viz., national or global.

Therefore, the travel from Socialism to Sarvodaya involves the participation of every individual and his welfare. As Gandhi put it, *"I do not believe...that an individual may gain spiritually and those who surround him suffer. I believe in advaita, I believe in the essential unity of man and, for that matter, of all that life's. Therefore, I believe that if one man gains spiritually, the whole world gains with him and, if one man falls, the whole world falls to that extent."*

Today, Sarvodaya must be an attribute of individual rights. For a common goal, voice of an individual should propagate along all others surround him. One who duly performs his duties alone can acquire the right to perform his duties. Keeping the welfare of the people as the central fulcrum of the cause, accruing the rights to perform duties is much worthier than anything in the life. The *"rise of all"* shall not clash with the *"welfare of all"*. If at all it happens, it would be a menace. *"The capitalist and the zamindar talk of their rights, the labourer on the other hand of his, the prince of his divine right to rule, the rioter of his to resist it. If all simply insist on rights and no duties, there will be utter confusion and chaos,"* Gandhi stated.

In a country of billions of people, everyone is aspiring for their rights to be fulfilled; duties to be accomplished. In order to serve them all, Sarvodaya must be the central theme behind their seeking. One shall not go with the utilitarian formula that speaks of the 'greatest good of the greatest number.' Greatest good of all must be the goal even at the cost of his life. And, that would be the moral realization of Sarvodaya. *"The greatest good of all inevitably includes the good of the greatest number, and therefore, he and the utilitarian will converge in many points in their career, but there does come a time when they must part company, and even work in opposite directions. The utilitarian to be logical will never sacrifice himself. The absolutist will even sacrifice himself."* Gandhi remained as an absolutist till the end. He served for the cause of greatest good bringing other utilitarian goods to converge into his scheme of Sarvodaya. For that to ensue successfully, he led not just a freedom movement but also a cooperative movement.

'India against Corruption' movement is a perfect example for the greatest good of all. Anna Hazare's Satyagraha forced the government to introduce LokPal in Parliament and when the same movement transformed politically in to a party, he refrained from it. His readiness to sacrifice for the cause of general good has ended successfully with no victory either for utilitarian or absolutist formula. But it was everyone's victory. The convergence between him and the government happened many times, but he parted away from the logical end unlike what ordinary men might have done. He preferred to stay out of the utilitarian whims. For the betterment of governance, Gandhi's idea of welfare of all is seen as a basement to construct other structures and systems so as to ensure that all is well.

"They say means are after all means, I would say means are after all everything. As the means, so the end...There is no wall or separation between means and end."[9] What we all need is *"True economics that stands for social justice; promoting the good of all equally including the weakest, and is indispensable for decent life."* Therefore, on the premises of Sarvodaya we must strive for the establishment of a new politico-economic order that encompasses the integrated welfare of each and every person.

Basis and need for Sarvodaya

In the pursuit of Truth, that is God, man continues to travel all across everywhere and experience the glimpses of God in His creations. The real truth could not be found in idolization or re-formation of God's nature. All along his path for the search of Truth (God), he embraces different schools of thought, various methods and modalities to see God. His desire and pursuit for the goal of realization of God, he needs guidance and enlightenment to carry out other aspects of life. Regrettably except a few monks and saints, we normal humans failed to meet this end of God realization.

Gandhi's pursuit of truth (God) was in finding God in man. He transformed himself to the lowliest of the human kind as he carried out his public life. Sarvodaya came out as a result of this understanding of Truth and God. He believed that Kingdom of God is within each and every individual. Ruskin's "Unto the Last" instantaneously transformed him to the degree of the translating that book in Gujarati entitled as "Sarvodaya" by Gandhi. *"Man's ultimate aim is the realization of God, and all his activities, social, political, religious, have to be guided by the ultimate aim of the vision of God. The immediate service of all human beings becomes a necessary part of the endeavour simply because the only way to find God is to see Him in His creation and be one with it. This can only be done by service of all."*

So, when nobody was there to till the soil, there a farmer. When nobody was to there to take care of cattle, there a shepherd; and when nobody was there to see God, there a service. Service to humanity is service to God. One must loose oneself in the service of humanity. For Gandhi, God was not in temples, churches or mosques or any other holy shrines. God was not in high skies and mountains, vast oceans and dense woods. He saw Him only in the human form and in service to him. *"I am a part and parcel of the whole and I cannot find Him apart from the rest of humanity. My countrymen are my nearest neighbours. They have become so helpless, so resource-less, so inert that I must concentrate myself on serving them. If I could persuade myself that I could find Him in a Himalayan cave, I would proceed there immediately. But I know that I cannot find Him apart from humanity."*

Thus, heartfelt service to poor identifies God within him. The smile of the poor who received the service is nothing but the smile of God. By serving the poor, one identifies himself. One cold realize the presence of God in that service. Through service to humanity, Gandhi did the service of country. He identified with every one of them he served. He could not differentiate him and the poor. His welfare is his welfare.

He wrote in Young India, *"Whenever I see an erring man, I say to myself I have also erred; when I see a lustful man, I say to myself so was I once; and in this way, I feel kinship with everyone in the world and feel that I cannot be happy without the humblest of us being happy."*

Gandhian deliberation towards solving International Conflicts

Overview

The world sees nonviolence as a tool for its balanced life of its inhabitants and for their over-all security. Individuals, Institutions and great persons continue to preach nonviolence and peace as the means to survive and live amicably in the worldly matters. Nevertheless, the inequalities and variations in the inherent capacities of people and nations comprising various religion, race and culture put the world in despair in the form of conflicts and wars.

Growing development of nuclear weapons by Iran, North Korea, Israel and other countries has triggered a new wave of threat in the international communities. Nuclear tests and researches are also not an exception from the list of warfare techniques that poses danger to the world's peace and global economic and diplomatic activities. Pakistan, being an Islamic state, is meting out terror outfits and Islamic fundamentalists along the Indian borders destabilizing peace in the region.

It explores the possible ways of Gandhian approach towards solving contemporary conflicts among the warring nations especially the conflicting interests of the U.S with Iran and North Korea. It also emphasizes how adhering to nonviolent tactics by the nations could avert a possible Third World War-like situations. And finally, it throws some light on internationalizing the Kashmir problem by the forces that knit a web of diplomatic, military and religious conflicts in Indo-Pak Border States. A nonviolent fight between nonviolence and the threatening forces like nuclear bombs and terror has been a challenging task before the world and recounts how Mahatma Gandhi's nonviolent ideology helps the world in upholding peace and harmony in resolving conflicts.

Introduction

What is challenging the world today is undoubtedly 'peace'. Peace has been constantly disturbed and defied by nations when their priorities change towards self-interested, greedy ways of doing day-to-day affairs. Poverty, lack of knowledge and education stands at the top of the list of factors that perturb peace triggering violent struggles and warfare. Ethnic clashes, economic differences, bullying of smaller nations by bigger ones and looting of wealth by intrusion are some other common factors that cause turbulence in the world of peace and nonviolence.

Peace among the nations is governed and sustained by a set of rules for nations to cooperate and co-exist among themselves despite differences in their race, culture, color, religion and ethnic origins. Many a leaders such as Mother Theresa, Dalai Lama, Abraham Lincoln, Theodore Roosevelt, Martin Luther King Jr, Nelson Mandela, Desmond Tutu, Mikhail Gorbachev etc., have served as standing role models for upholding peace and nonviolence in the world by putting keen efforts to maintain peace among the nations at times of conflict. Several organizations such as the United Nations, Red Cross, Institute of International Law, International

Atomic Energy Agency, Amnesty International and International Campaign to abolish Nuclear Weapons etc have contributed their efforts to uphold humanity and harmony among the nations preventing wars and massive destruction by lethal weapons. Many a philosophers like Aristotle, Plato, G.K.Chesterton, Confucius, Guru Nanak, Solomon, Lao Tzu etc., have all had their preaching to the world with the basis of love and peace as a way of living for the entire human kind. Nevertheless, Mahatma Gandhi is one of the tallest leader, philosopher and an institution by himself who demonstrated peace and nonviolence in a comprehensive way of organizing the society and politic with his doctrine of "Ahimsa" and peasants' power of democracy. His speeches and writings have become a set of guidelines serving as a base for building economy, governance, legal infrastructure and social organization.

More significantly his principles and methods have gained roots in the global politics and governance giving the world a chance to restore and revamp the broken societies, wrecked economies and tarnished governances. The world now sees Gandhi as a means to imbibe a new culture of peace and non-violence more than ever before. People elsewhere have understood the need for nonviolence as a tool for tackling the conflicts, big and small, giving them a chance for upholding their rights, freedom and duties. His doctrine of nonviolence provides them a methodological approach in dealing with their issues and problems even as the world is trying to prevent war and crimes to the lowest in numbers. Gandhi stands as a tall figure spreading a wave of peace and harmony in the souls and minds providing happiness, glow and brilliance in leadership and direction towards attaining the goals, roles and responsibilities one has to acquire by systematic ways; Needless to mention the personal transformation and various inspiring forms emerging out of Gandhi. Today's Gandhism and various manifestations of Gandhi have been contributing the world with its excellence in ideological applications and followership.

Notwithstanding the awareness and significance of peace, love and nonviolence in the world, there erupts a manifold occurrence of terror, crime, violence and war in parts of the world. Owing to these conflicting interests of the world, there exists a lot of deceitful motives unfair rationale and odd grounds between the countries in trade, commerce and diplomatic relations. The United States of America is one among the developed countries, which has been constantly having rough ties with the emerging powers and developing nations, tries to dictate terms of accordance and adherence to international laws in its own way of nonviolent, peaceful approaches to countries like Iran, North Korea and Pakistan. While these countries have their own way of origin, existence and development for centuries, only in the later part of 20th century they seemed to gain global importance and spread their policies successfully worldwide what the U.S. has understood and interpreted as immoralist and breaching the global standards. The conflict and fight between these countries and the U.S. has baffled the whole world hurting the communities, throttling the economies and disbanding the orderliness in political structures.

Gandhi and Conflict Resolution

The science of conflict resolution comprises the implementation of processes and methods leading to a peaceful settlement of any disagreement, ending the conflict on a permanent basis. Communicating the interests and motives of one group to another through the means of the methods like negotiation, mediation, diplomacy, and creative peace building would result into initiation of nonviolent measures yielding a better, effective resolution.

It has been discovered that the science of conflict resolution is repeatedly misconstrued and immaterialized in its entirety. Hence, the world is yet to see an irrefutable, distinguishing character which, by practice, stands as a perfect icon on its own with a sole exception of Mahatma Gandhi. Gandhi in his lifetime, in fact, he dedicated whole of his life for the resolution of conflicts surfaced from the various heads of the states, governments and the people. The correlation and application of methods of conflict resolution by Gandhi in his days is impeccable enough to define both the disciplines of conflict management and resolution. Portraying Gandhi as a master of conflict resolution, who through his nonviolent, non-cooperative methods combined with the huge support of the masses in his freedom movement, is inevitable for the reason that he had applied all of the possible resolution techniques at some point or the other in his lifetime.

Gandhi, as a conflict resolver used the interest based approach by fostering direct communication with disputants, solving issues, and drafting agreements to meet their fundamental needs. The indentured labourers of India in South Africa formed the key client base for his legal profession, through which he had successfully advocated his philosophy of life, using which later gave a wonderful shape to the freedom movement in the form of nonviolence, Satyagraha, truth and justice. In his efforts for upholding truth, justice, he as a conflict resolver, sought after rulings such as finding a win-win solution, or mutually satisfying scenario, or for everyone's welfare, or "getting to yes" type of resolutions.

The science of conflict resolution suggest that there are five conflict resolution styles/strategies that one may use depending on his outlook toward pro-self or pro-social goals: They are: Avoidance, Yielding, Competitive, Cooperation, and Conciliation. When these tactics applied on the current crisis and conflict between the U.S. and Iran, North Korea and Pakistan from a Gandhian point of view, hope things would change to normal. The combined understanding of Gandhian approach and the conflict resolution strategies would bring an atmosphere of peace and harmony in the diplomatic and political circles of these countries. A goad of Gandhian thoughts inside the diplomatic framework would enable peace in international ties. For this to happen, the offices of the foreign relations shall have to provide a space for understanding the strategic, nonviolent and focused system within their hemisphere.

The U.S. and Iran conflict

Ironically, when looked at the history of Iran-U.S. relations, one can find how both the nations have been partners on many occasions and maintained it through trade and cultural exchanges. Iran, being a small mid-east country has been ruled by the pro-American Shah until the Iranian revolution in 1979 that ousted him from power. Replaced by the religious leader Ayatollah Ali Khamenei, Iran has been projecting itself as an Islamic state pushing the state of the affairs into disorder raising multiple questions to its citizen from control of power to internal governance to foreign relations. The U.S., its trustworthy partner had been put into a state of muddle as the student groups and democratic forces continue to occupy the embassy in Teheran raising anti-American slogan. It was the time in 1980's when Iran's foreign policy was at its very low as diplomacy was run and controlled by democracy.

When the U.S. began to impose sanctions, Iran's trade suffered a bit escalating the conflict that reflected in the neighboring countries and the rest of the world as well. The U.S. has become a *"troubling master"* for Iran and the latter became a *"rough and self-styled"* nation. Iran began to shift its trade and commerce away from the U.S.

even as it began to start buying nuclear weapons and conducting nuclear tests.

The military aspects of the Iran also have turned into ugly state of affairs when Iran has successfully sustained and transformed into *"independent"* state with its anti-American stance. And of late, Iranian officials vowed to fight the U.S. aggression defending its borders even as an Iranian missile shot down a U.S. Global Hawk Surveillance Drone in June 2019. The U.S. also maintains its firm stance of confront as President Donald Trump reiterated that his government would impose new sanctions on Iran. What is notable here is that the President has said that he aborted a military strike as retaliation to the Iran's downing of the drone but willing to deliberate and continue talks to settle the issues.

One has to feebly notice the U.S. government and the President has been trying to *"normalize"* the Iran's recent developments while the mid-east country continues to sail across the global seas *"in its own way."* Along with the executive order imposing the sanctions on Iran, the statement from the President reads, "We call on the regime to abandon its nuclear ambitions, change its destructive behavior, respect the rights of its people, and return in good faith to the negotiating table."

Iran's fighting attitude with the U.S. and its aspiration to become *"another"* power may be inevitable with all its developmental efforts despite its small size. Its competitive approach may be a welcome one as long as it adheres to a popular note from Gandhi, *"Man's nature is not essentially evil. Brute nature has been known to yield to the influence of love. You must never despair of human nature."* The U.S. must also realize the fact that *"Forgiveness is the attribute of the strong."*

The U.S. and North Korea

On June 30, 2019, U.S. President Donald Trump visited North Korean leader Kim Jong-Un at the Joint Security Area along the borders as an important step towards denuclearizing the Korean Peninsula. The South Korean President Moon Jae-in also accompanied the U.S. President on this visit in the middle of a long truce between the two Korean nations raging in to differences among themselves due to U.S. and Soviet inclinations. Even as the South Koreans received support from the U.S., North Korea has been since its partition, governed by the Soviet pressures, Japanese occupation and mass opposition to the U.S.

One of the root causes of souring relationship between the two nations is the inclusion of Korea in Japan's sphere of influence and the subsequent annexure of Korea by Japan in 1905. Tensions mounted only to see Korea divided with the help of the United Nations after the World War II. The U.S. was not given due respect even as North Korea was declared as Democratic People's Republic of Korea. The growing recognition of North Korea by Soviet Union distanced the U.S. from the people of North Korea. Thus the Korean peninsula has been caught in a web of *"friendship priorities"* that ruined the state of the affairs which pulled military actions into force not only between the North and South Koreas but also from the U.S.

After the series of killings of the U.S. soldiers on occupation in the North Korean borders, the relations severed heavily during the period 1950-1990s. It was almost an armistice and peaceful sailing for North Korea until it was found to be verified by the Bill Clinton's administration on the suspicion of producing plutonium and building nuclear bombs. America, in its *"watchman of the world"* role, determined to denuclearize North

Korea at the risk of possible war. Both the nations attacked each other's helicopters and shipments across their seas. Tensions shoot up when North Korea was cornered with money laundering charges in 2005. Only in 2007 during the Bush Administration, diplomatic relationship began to be pleasing after the Six Party talks that built a new regional peace structure for North Korea. Subsequently, North Korea shut down its Yongbyon Nuclear facility to remove its name from the list of state sponsors of terrorism.

The political and military actions between the U.S. and North Korea have been a matter of avoidance and conciliation style of conflict resolution. The Korean nation wants to avoid the U.S. while the latter wants to reconcile despite cultural inequalities and diverse allies. *"A 'No' uttered from the deepest conviction is better than a 'Yes' merely uttered to please, or worse, to avoid trouble."* George Orwell pointed out in his Reflections of Gandhi, "…as a Nationalist, he was an enemy, but since in every crisis he would exert himself to prevent violence…" North Korea has befriended with many Asian nations due its avoidance of the U.S. but while safeguarding itself from the aggressive U.S. conciliation, could not prevent violence. On the other hand, the U.S.

attempts to reconciliation with North Korea must have been little gracious enough to create a congenial atmosphere in the Korean peninsula.

"An eye for an eye will only make the whole world blind." Back-to-back nuclear testing and proliferation of nuclear weapons would enhance the rivalry not only with the U.S. but also with other countries. North Korea may have to learn from its south for focusing on development and progress setting aside the military outlook on relations with the U.S. It may not indulge in activities to woo the attraction from the U.S. or any other country to exhibit its supremacy in the region for the reason the Soviet and Japanese influence over the Korean peninsula might not long last. Freedom and liberty of the people of Korea rests with the responsibility of Korean administration.

The North Korean nuclear threat has not only provoked the Americans, but also the countries that are in good relationship with the U.S. The Trump government has not yet taken any adverse reaction to North Korea. Peace lovers and nonviolent activists across the world have been deeply apprehended by the changing conditions in the global nuclear race. Peace activism, Gandhian approaches and nonviolent strategies shall be given due importance as a means to avert war and violence at first place, rather seen as an act of post-mortem effort. As Gandhi stated, *"It is a first class human tragedy that people of the earth who claim to believe in the message of Jesus, whom they describe as the Prince of Peace, show little of that belief in actual practice."*

North Korean leader Kim Jong-Un has been instigating the southern Korea and the U.S by constant disclosure of his nuclear capabilities by inspecting submarines, launching missiles and developing nuclear weapons. North Korea's problems of today are greatly attributed to this young leader. Being an unelected dictator and frequent violator of human rights, Kim Jong-Un has been in the recent news for his actions that disconnect him from rest of the countries. It is becoming increasingly hard for other countries including the U.S. to step up trade and commerce and other economic treaties. Diplomatic strategies of co-operation and conciliation that are required for resolving conflict have been weakened because of the tainted leadership.

Gandhi believed, *"The personal creed of a non-co-operator does not preclude him from representing the cause of those who are helplessly cooperators."* It is either change in leadership or personal transformation of the leadership might bring better bonding with North Korea.

It is not the King alone thrives and civilians get killed during a war or conflict. It is not the King alone die and only civilians rule at times of conflict. It needs a public will along with a conducive environment to lead and live a nation. Gandhi's *Sarvodaya* meant "development of all" through *Antyodaya,* implying the welfare of all through the weakest of the society implementing the principles of cooperation and collective endeavor which are central to any society. According to him, *Sarvodaya* is not the politics of power but the politics of cooperation.

In his later years, Gandhi said, *"...I was a co-operator too in the sense that I non-co-operated for co-operation, and even then I said that if I could carry the country forward by co-operation I should co-operate."* And that is the message.

India and Pakistan

During the creation of India and Pakistan in 1947, almost 261 provinces came into unification plan leaving aside the state of Kashmir which had a Muslim majority ruled by Hindu king. Pakistan was eyeing at its Muslim population with a dream of acquisition of Kashmir. India took its stance as a commander of the princely states hoping to bring them all into one except certain parts of Kashmir.

In his freedom struggle movement, one could observe a unique "accommodating" style of conflict resolution in Gandhi which displayed his character of high concern for others while having a low concern for his own self. While he was seen as the leader of the majority Hindus, he believed that there needed a Muslim League to represent minority Muslims. The co-creation of India and Pakistan accommodated both the Hindus and Muslims in his crusade against the British Raj. Despite the critical views of other leaders like Rajaji, Patel, he invited Jinnah's opinion on many occasions and placed the leagues' manifest in the congress committee.

In his talks for United India, he emphatically pleaded Jinnah, "...*If you do not agree to these terms, could you let me know in precise terms what you would have me accept in terms of the Lahore Resolution and bind myself to recommend to the Congress?*" "*...Whenever you are confronted with an opponent, conquer him with love.*" It is the best way to find cooperation from others as well.

His fast-unto-deaths have put both the factions into a state of hollowness, but diluting the whole conflict, bringing harmony. The talks between Gandhi and Jinnah are highly valued in the history of the world as it brought an end to the long lasting scuffle in the Indian subcontinent and it stands today as a *wise* example for conflict resolution. Rebel leaders suspected the resolution of partition of India as of managing a situational crisis rather than a permanent solution. Do anyone think of a rather, better solution for this issue at the juncture of achieving freedom for a nation? The conflicts occurring from time to time between India and Pakistan nowadays are, in general, hailed as the "most sought after state of affairs" preferred by people of both the religions and nations. In fact, the partition of India stands as a foundation for the use of Gandhian model for setting up of foreign relations.

Pakistan's persistent efforts to invade Kashmir were defeated by India in four wars since 1947 that severed tensions and instability not only within the civilians, but also with the military forces of both the nations. Frequent attacks on convoys and military installations across the line of border between India and Pakistan have escalated the fire of animosity between them.

Even as India continued its stance of not attacking or warring with her neighbor, Pakistan, being an Islamic country, is meting out terror outfits and Islamic fundamentalists along the Indian borders creating bloodshed and tension. War between Pakistan and India has has not that much militarized and formalized since the rage is between religious groups and the growing Islamic sentiments. Attacks and war with Pakistan surely is a blot on India's democracy, peace and its secular state.

Diplomatic ties between Pakistan and India seems to be sailing smoother and more than usual after Agra Summit in 2001. Talks at higher levels, exchange of prisoners, bus and train transportation and regular meetings amongst the ministers of both the nations - are certain measures that diplomacy have seen in the last decade. Unstable governments, corrupt leaders, and in-state violence and terror attacks detached Pakistan from healthy state of diplomatic affairs with India.

High commissions and embassies run for namesake just to promote little peace left with cultural programs, trade and commerce. With the advent of the new government formed in Pakistan headed by Mr. Imran Khan, things have not improved, rather hanging on air.

For both India and Pakistan the religious divide alone shall not be a barrier to maintain peace in the region. It is the un-resolved, disputed region that triggers the violent mood of the religious forces. A clear mandate shall be arrived in near future to sort out the conflicting issues; it shall be more of a democratic process, rather not a diplomatic or military action that could bring peace in Kashmir.

Conclusion

The world is running in harmony as per cords that bind all of us synchronously through cultural, technological, economic and by commercial terms and conditions. A war would mean a big blow to both the developed and the developing nations. A war is an evil. It brings destruction and ruins. It confiscates the lives from normal track of life. The third World War is not going to be the same as I and II. The egotist supremacy in the global relations and politics, race for seizing the top-most place of power and the challenging of existing power centers – are now equipped with nuclear and chemical weapons that could destroy the world in seconds. The first two Great wars had not seen such a vast range of weapons and techniques what the military have today.

The Third World War has been spoken for many decades, in theory and in news. Global peace might be at risk; it might be just another choice for some. Peace might be farther than what the world has pondered it over the centuries. Nevertheless, the world is still busy with other *'important'* things, not with the war. Hope the faith the world has put on peace lives forever.

And, this faith must transcends down from one nation to another. It is important for nations to take note of how much of importance been given to their nonviolent approaches along side the nuclear actions they perform even if they are meant for energy purposes. For a nation, economic growth is directly proportional to the rise in their arms reserves. Security and mutual respect are a serious concern which demands cordial relationship among the nations. Global security and reconciliation must be the direct outcome of any steps taken towards resolving conflicts between the nations.

"While hatred is the main cause of violence, there won't be space for tolerance. While tolerance is interpreted as

injustice, there won't be space for nonviolence. When ignorance is exploited across the poor sections of the society, there won't be space for truth and justice. When basic ground rules are violated by authorities, there exists a space for the vested ones. While vested interests take charge of power, there won't be space for conflict resolution." Keeping this as a central tenet for maintaining global peace, nations must aim to work for resolving international conflicts. The world shall have to ponder over its choices rather than challenging the rivals to resolve conflicts.

Localized Economy

Abstract

"If the village perishes, India will perish too. It will be no more India. Her own mission in the world will get lost." What Gandhi really meant when he talked about village swaraj and village industries? Do our villages constitute the character of the village what Gandhi dreamt?

Here I try to explore the characteristics and power of village swaraj and village industries what I collectively call it as "Localized economy" in the context of today's economy. Supplying of raw materials and manufacturing of semi-finished or un-finished goods for bigger industries constitute the localized economy. It also consists of setting up of smaller units of production of goods that serve the basic needs of the local or rural economic region.

Today, localized economy is being globalized and privatized in a fast pace forbidding the human and moral factors in villages. I emphasize the need for limited machinery and increased focus towards human development and human participation in building economies. It also throws some light towards finding the ways to attain the goals of localized economy what Gandhi stated. Comparing today's economy, be it local or global, with that of moral economics of Gandhi would enlighten us the direction in which we take our economy towards future. And finally, there is an analysis on the social impact caused by today's economic activities going on in the remote villages.

∞∞ 𝔜 𝔜 𝔜 ∞∞

Overview

"The Earth provides enough to satisfy every man's need but not every man's greed." This famous passage by Gandhiji is not to be construed at global perspective. It holds good even for the localized, community-level economic growth as well. One man shall not thrive for his own good and neither shall he put all his efforts for the common good. The collective growth and development is the key for the success of any local economy. Gandhiji's 'Village Swaraj' brings us a concept of having a certain geographical unit of land with its own social, economic and government structure linked to natural resources within the specified boundaries. A typical village will have everything an individual wants including food, clothing, school, theatre, public hall, health care facilities etc. But many times a village cannot thrive on its private

resources, but inter-dependent on neighbouring villages. A self-reliant, localized economy shall be achieved only with the unification of a few number of villages and governed collectively as a single unit.

Every such region shall serve as a centre for enabling and experiencing the socio-cultural needs and have economic development programs to sustain the growing needs of the region. The collective approach at the local or rural economic region will thus facilitate the never-ending search for the infrastructural requirements and resources that puts us in building rural economy.

Man versus Machine

Gandhi was once asked, "Are you against this machine age?" Gandhi replied, "To *say that is to caricature my views. I am not against machinery as such, but I am totally opposed to it when it masters us*." "Are you against industrializing India?" He put it so clearly saying, "*The village communities should be revived. Indian villages produced and supplied to the Indian towns and cities all their wants. India became impoverished when our cities became foreign markets and began to drain the villages dry by dumping cheap and shoddy goods from foreign lands.*"

"Village Swaraj is man-centred, non-exploiting, decentralized, simple village economy providing for full employment to each one of its citizens on the basis of voluntary co-operation and working for achieving self-sufficiency in its basic requirements of food, clothing and other necessities of life. To build such a non-violent economy providing for full employment of all citizens he ruled out industrialism, centralized industries and unnecessary machinery." - H.M. Vyas, 1962

Gandhi believed that *exploitation is the essence of violence*. He perceived that the imperial governance and economic conditions of the Indians are directly correlated. The technique of the British in provoking people violently and governing them rudely in reciprocation had been the order of the day. Their undue taxation, atrocities in governing individual's properties and wealth, and exhibiting supremacy over the natives had had put the whole country burning with violent fumes if not otherwise suppressed the people to a clout of slavery. Gandhi's ahimsa addressed not only those arrogant rulers but also the peasants and people who were on the verge of breaking aggressively to combat the exploitative situation present in the country.

Decentralization has happened globally. Multinational companies have set up their units in villages promoting localized economy. But, control of power and administration remains at the top-level management who take decisions drinking chocolate in NewYork or Tokyo. This is not the true village swaraj or village economy what Gandhi built.

He diverted the people's energy and power to build constructive work. He steered the spinning with charka as a mantra across the country for mass production and human unity that could pose a challenging spirit against the imperial industries and importing of goods. His protests for boycotting foreign clothes and neglect of mill workers were not just the symbols of independence movement, but signified his vision for building localized economy. His campaign for charka spinning and traditional methods of weaving satisfied the economic needs of the rural poor. He believed that the economic self-reliance of thousands of villages in India would bring self-rule of the nation as a whole.

Moral Economy

"Economics that hurt the moral wellbeing of an individual or a nation are immoral and therefore sinful. Thus, the economics that permit one country to prey upon another are immoral. It is sinful to buy and use articles made by sweated labour." Chinese goods and imported goods are on the rise. Governments didn't seem to stop the policies that hurt the moral being of our lives. While trade policies and tax structures are targeting the manufacturers and distributors, consumers are left with no choice except to go for buying things that are borne out of other's labour and sweat. Indigenous production is the only means to uphold the moral nature of people.

"The economics that disregard moral and sentimental considerations are like wax works that being life-like still lack the life of the living flesh. At every crucial moment these new-fangled economic laws have broken down in practice. And nations or individuals who accept them as guiding maxims must perish." Governments are trying to bring up the falling economy by means of new-fangled economic laws like merging of banks and banning of currency notes which turn out to be nothing but digging its own grave. More focus is given to statistical figures like growth rate, GDP, Rupee value, unemployment rate

etc., but not the degrading human values and moral upholding in the society as a whole.

For Gandhi, *"The extension of the law of non-violence in the domain of economics means nothing less than the introduction of moral values as a factor to be considered in regulating international commerce."* Today, international commerce has been condensed into multi-billion dollar projects and tie-ups that showcase the detrimental needs of the society and nothing less than the luxurious, westernization that degrades Indian lifestyle. Smaller and medium-sized Indian companies are shutting down as economy stands over multi-national franchising and foreign exchanges. Industries continue to adopt foreign technologies and machinery by setting up of assembly units that works for the economic growth in a shorter period of time but it so happened by costing the morality, natural resources and culture of the region.

For Gandhi, *"The study of Indian economics is the study of the spinning wheel.* Today's economy is study and practice of Digital India. Computers and mobiles have become the central theme behind all businesses including rural production, agriculture and manufacturing sectors.

For Gandhi, *"Religion to be true must satisfy what may be termed humanitarian economics, that is, where the income and the expenditure balance each other."* Today's religion is the brutality of cow rakshakas and balancing the politics of vengeance by killing innocent Hindus and Muslims in equal numbers. Equality remains only in hurting the sentiments of all religions. Tit for tat kind of fight amongst all religions is not the way for balancing the humanitarian economics. Rather equality of religions must pave the way for building collective growth and sharing of economic development. The Supreme Court verdict in 2019 on Ram Janmabhoomi case stated that the existing site must be owned by Hindus to build Ram Mandir whereas five acres of land would be allotted to Muslims for building a mosque. The judgment might be seen as a testament for Gandhian economics as it resolves both the religious conflict and satisfy the humanitarian economics to some extent.

Localized Economy and Society

Over the last two decades, Indian villages have witnessed a series of development through various policies and promotional efforts from the government in the name of economic reforms. Private industries, corporate offices, educational institutions and research centres have cropped up in remote villages. Today, villages have access to satellite communication, wireless, Internet technologies, world-class schools, colleges, roads, transportation and educational facilities besides playing an important role in hosting their large vacant lands for setting up of multi-national companies and factories. Do all these constitute a localized economy what Gandhi had dreamed? Definitely not.

The Localized economy what villages see today has been alarming and threatening to its very own existence. Village developments happen at the cost of arable lands, human values and inherent values the villages possess. One may not immediately notice the serious damage that has been caused at the social level due to these economic activities and restructuring of villages. Not that this apprehension be discussed in the perception of westernization factor that has involved in these economic developments but the alterations occurred in the inherent social structure, values and belief existing in the society. Critical analysts and activists, pointing at the gradual declining of ethical values and social principles, are more bothered about the impact of economic activities on the conventional morality of the people.

For instance, when Tatas wanted to establish their plant in Singur, West Bengal, a remote village off 300 kilometers from Kolkata, the traditional value of the land came into controversy. The benefits such as economic growth, standard of life, job opportunities and modernization of the area were given less consideration by the local people. It is not the value of the land in rupees that mattered but the moralistic worth and cultural heritage of the land that stood with the sons of the soil which came in the middle of that economic development. Industrialization in remote villages, so long been left as arid land used for nothing, is considered as a reformation and renovation of economy. But the society that is carved in and out of that industrialization merely reflects a large gathering of lives settled for work, food and enjoyment in spiteful ways. In real terms, it is not a society at all. It is a way of life newly created which might have no value of civilization, culture, tradition or ethnicity. Villages take part in an economy to match with the so-called global standards not the inherent values or the standards created out of their own brains. Villages accommodate modern ways of living and work culture while people are gradually becoming neo-modern, state-less citizens. Current developments in villages put the state and condition of the rural people in jeopardy persuading their life-search towards coercive global opportunities.

Economies built on the code of ethics alone can serve the society. As Mahatma Gandhi emphatically noted, "*Commerce without morality*" is a sin. The economy that resulted out of such unfair trade and commerce practices might surely be considered as a social evil rather than been acclaimed as a social upliftment. Our villages are no more a village but a mix-up of semi-urbanization and eroded rural community. Our village economy is not at all an economy that sustains our lives and the country, but a superficial economic activity that rolls over the villages damaging peace, culture and ethnicity. Village people are lost in their own world. The beliefs are slowly withering away as the values are disregarded in the process of mechanization of life and work. Machines do all the work and social minds get occupied with the superfluous manipulations on money, mankind and markets. Social gatherings and person to person contacts have diminished to become a more simple form of networking through computers. Citizens have become Netizens.

Gandhi's economic vision was aimed at the removal of - exploitation, economic inequality and a world order based on war. He conceptualized the ideas of cooperation and sharing, universal participation in physical labour, voluntary limitation of wants, decentralization of economic activities, a new technology called "*Swadeshi*" in consonance with the new goals, and the transformation of private ownership into trusteeship. Gandhiji wanted to build social justice and welfare amalgamated with economy where as today's economic policies dictate terms on its own, not evolving out of any social means but for political pragmatism. Our villages must be willing to accommodate economic activities following such principles.

Summary

To strengthen and propagate such a nonviolent economic theme, it has to be universalized. We need to establish high end research and educational support for such internationalization. Localized economy has become a key driving factor for global economy also. The wide gap between the rural management programmes and the conventional management techniques need to be identified and filled up by setting up resource centres in the villages. The philosophy, culture, art and science, business management of the primitives in the villages need to be secured and preserved as a treasure so as to ensure the heritage and integrity of the nation. Villages shall not be swept away simply by the blowing wind of the western mobilization and impact formed out of globalization.

It needs a consistent effort from the government and various organizations in developing village programs to ensure the empowerment of social, political and economic aspects among the poor and the deprived. The localized economy flourishes by empowering the poor, under-privileged and un-served people and areas and a qualitative improvement as an immediate effect can be seen in many regions. The income generation activities by women groups, self-help groups and the youth groups are becoming common among the rural public. Villagers are keen to know more about their environment and learn to campaign on any critical issues that damages the environment. The village economy is the nonviolent economy for the poor and building the one in a moralistic, self-reliant way is a service to humanity. It is the economy that brings economic equality.

"What exactly do you mean by economic equality," Gandhiji was asked at the Constructive Worker's Conference during his tour of Madras. Gandhiji's reply was that *economic equality of his conception did not mean that everyone would literally have the same amount. It simply meant that everybody should have enough for his or her needs.* Localized economy must be aimed towards achieving the economic equality. Village industries, their production, distribution and consumption – all must be matching with that of what industries do in cities and towns. Thus, localized economy will become a separate compartment working autonomously to serve the masses. *Under Gandhian economic order, the character of production will be determined by social necessity and not by personal whim or greed.*

Developmental impact on Environment

Overview

Market development in India is dynamic and inconsistent. Most of the markets - oil, gold, electronics, infrastructure and technological equipments – depend on the surge and fall of respective economies at the global markets. India is becoming more and more inter-dependent in this post-globalization era. While the global markets claim that environmental factors are very much under control and examination to safeguard environment, there still exists a big question: Do markets really do justice to the environment as they continue to develop and diversify in these days?

Here I try to explore the market environment as it is and with a Gandhian perspective diving deeper in to factors that are correlated to market development and environmental protection. Gandhian economic model with a focus on local production and localized markets is also discussed in detail to establish how that model came as a solution for most of the problems we face in today's development.

When Gandhi said, *"India became impoverished when our cities became foreign markets and began to drain the villages dry by dumping cheap and shoddy goods from foreign lands,"* it doesn't just imply that markets are being polluted by scrap imported but also the environmental change and impact it created. It explores the recent draft of the Environmental Impact Assessment (EIA) in connotation with Gandhian model of development and environmental conservation. It checks if the Gandhian economic vision has been met with new methods of development keeping environment as the central focus of discussion.

Economic Development

Economic development is the process of transforming simple, low-income national economies into modern industrial economies. A country's per capita income is the best available measure of the value of goods and services available per person, to the society per year. Economic well-being of a country is determined by the rate of growth in this factor. And, this is correlated to other factors such as life-expectancy, infant mortality rates, health and nutrition and literacy rates. Lower per capita income level is an index of poverty which is by other means interpreted as lower per capita consumption and worsened standards of living.

Market economy is an economic system in which the decisions regarding investment, production and distribution are guided by the price signals created by forces of demand and supply.

Every government has a responsible role in keeping its market economy at par with its economic growth meaning that state-controlled economic activities determine the economic development of the country. Market pricing, market failures, public distribution of goods and services, safeguarding private ownership – State plays a directive role in guiding the overall development of the market through industrial policies. Liberalization and globalization plans have thrown open doors of market development changing its size, flow of goods and services and stability. What is allowed and what not? What is appropriate and what not? What improves the living standards and what not? These questions are key determinants for how the sustainable economy is achieved.

Let us look at two resolutions made recently by the Government of India viz. Environmental Impact Assessment and National Green Tribunal in the following sections.

Environmental Impact Assessment (EIA)

Environmental Impact Assessment is a process of evaluating the likely environmental impacts of a proposed project or development, taking into account inter-related socio-economic, cultural and human –health impacts, beneficial and adverse. Our development and health – wherever the socio-economic activities involved – are dependent on a healthy environment.

EIA is supposed to create and sustain a regulatory framework that prevents the plunder of our natural resources, not actively accelerate the pace of environmental devastation. Just as the criterion affecting the nation's economic development, certain processes and guidelines would prove severely detrimental to the environment. The norms set for environmental clearance, environmental permission, and environmental rights, there needs to be environmental assessment that is sustainable, legal and of quality-proof standards maintaining balance between the proposed project and environment. While utmost care is taken in the interest of the project owners and developers to adhere to a simple, efficient, time-saving process, there needs more focus and importance attached to the expected outcome of the assessment. Compromising with environmental well-being at the advent of updated EIA procedure is unlikely to do any such welfare to the nation as a whole. There exists a layer of uncertainties and lack of clarity in assessing the environmental projects which causes to bring issues in future when the projects are on the run. The National Green Tribunal (NGT) would address the grievances and victimization of those projects flouting EIA procedures through legal means.

"The Earth provides enough to satisfy every man's need but not every man's greed." This famous passage by Gandhiji is not to be construed in a general perspective. It holds good even for the localized, community-level economic growth and the modern industrialized economy as well. One man shall not thrive for his own good and neither shall he put all his efforts for the common good. Industries flourished based on the theme of collective wealth and shared income. The collective growth and development is the key mantra in the market economy and economic development. Problems arise if a brand or

company tries to swallow the entire market and reign as a supreme monopoly. When governments implement the model of Gandhiji's 'Village Swaraj', industries seize over a certain geographical unit of land with its own social, economic and government structure linked to natural resources within the specified boundaries. Even though the technological parks and industrial development units operate within the framework of rural development, it is the foreign investments and foreign-handed operations that gets boosted by the governing polices. It may be easier for laying down the environmental policies to a foreign venture as it has to go through various permits to start business in India. For the purpose of earning more profits, rental taxes and all other incomes, natural resources have been directed towards foreign investments creating more such industrial plots out of the exploitation of natural landscapes. Nature thus utilized for the purpose of economic development in course of time generates other issues pertaining to the environment - from health to environment and social to economic.

Economic Development vs. Environment

India's per capita net income for the fiscal year 2020 is roughly around Rs. 135000. It is expected to fall by 5.4%

in the year 2021 due to Covid-19 pandemic. India's public sector enterprises and private entrepreneurship have been contributing to market development for many decades. Of late, government initiatives to establish state-owned enterprises in telecom and IT sectors have affected considerably the market size and pricing policies. In the pre-Covid-19 days, per capita income grew at the rate of 8.6%. Gross Domestic Product (GDP) index of India reached -3.2% in the beginning of the year 2020. It went down to -23.9 in mid 2020. Obviously, these figures reflect the declining state of wealth and affluence in the country.

When we look at the sector-wise GDP, agriculture contributes to 15.4%, industries 23% and services 61.5%. The measures and policies developed by the state seem to improvise the services sector more emphatically than the other two sectors. When it comes to investment, more and more funds and provisions are made for services. Economic systems are being derived from successful western models and when it gets implemented in our country the same has become irrelevant and failure. A great deal of harm has been done to agriculture sector. Vast extent of cultivable land has been plundered over the years due to population explosion and non-judicial use of resources. Much of natural degradation is happening at the community-level violations. Deforestation is happening at the rocket speed. Sand mining and depletion of water bodies are on the rise. Modernization of cities and urbanization of villages swallow greenery and arable lands.

Sustainable economy

The Brundtland Commission defined Sustainable Development in 1987 as that which *"meets the needs of the present without compromising the ability of the future generations to meet their own needs"*. It is important to view sustainable efforts from global perspective that addresses socio-economic and environmental issues. The Agenda21 drafted at the Rio Summit called all countries to develop national strategies for sustainable development to translate the words and commitments of Earth summit into concrete policies and actions. A primary goal of sustainable development is to achieve a reasonable and equitably distributed level of economic well being that can be perpetuated continually for many human generations. Thus, sustainability refers to the development with no side-effects on the socio-economic, cultural and human-health aspects of our life.

"Does moral progress increase in the same proportion as material progress?" This is not a question which has been in debate these days. Even in the days of Gandhi and Nehru, this was the issue to determine the viability of the progress of the nation under British Empire. Gandhi and Nehru have communicated through many letters on many occasions to emphasize village Swaraj and village economy through constructive programmes. His concept of Purna Swaraj included components such as communal unity, removal of untouchability, prohibition, development of village industries, renewable energy sources, village sanitation, new basic education, adult education, education in health and hygiene, promotion of provincial as well as national languages, economic equality, focus on the welfare of women, students, kisans, labourers and adivasis, the place of civil disobedience, and lastly khadi. To construct a model village comprising all of these, one needs basic knowledge and minimum technology what India possessed even in those days. On this possibility of a self-sustained village, he said: *"It's not too late at all. You just don't yet know what you are capable of."*

But, what we see today is a proactive development that focuses on mobilizing our economy quicker and put us in the global map in a fraction of second. The poor villages, lands and resources are being exploited by the foreign industries and also by our own countrymen and the city dwellers leaving the peasants no control over their own properties. We failed to work on our beliefs and values despite being a global society. We are unable to think for ourselves and therefore, allow multinationals and transnational corporations to dictate to us our wants, which led us confused with the actual needs. In Young India, Gandhiji stated that *"an increase in resources does nothing to increase welfare, since wants increase correspondingly. The extent to which existing demands are satisfied may never increase because wants rise commensurably with resources."* The infinite multiplicity of wants has put us on the technology-driven race, markets clustering like mushrooms and economy mixes.

His notion of people's buying behaviour, buying capacity and consumption pattern holds good even today when he stated *"Western nations today are groaning under the heel of the monster-god of materialism"* in his 25th December 1916 speech. And today, India and other Asian countries are blaming each other for becoming dumping yards of the west. Both industrial and retail markets filled with items that charm people destroying two main aspects of the society. One, the human nature being thwarted by the increased use of machines and tools and two, subsequent damage these items causing in the environment in the form of slip and scrap.

National Green Tribunal (NGT)

Most of the environmental damage caused in the country is due to industrial pollution. Industries and automobiles constitute 80% of the effluence and the rest is caused by human interventions. The National Green Tribunal was set up in 2010 to do some justice in dealing with environmental issues. India is third in the world, next to Australia and New Zealand, to set up a body to handle the environmental cases. Recently, the NGT has delivered a verdict that made illegal for vehicles over 15 years old run by diesel from plying on the roads of Delhi. To reduce air pollution, the State government has brought an odd-even system of plying vehicles with odd numbers one day and even numbers next. Environment is under serious risk by the fact that four hundred cases have been filed in the tribunal up till the month of June 202, at least.

In Chattisgarh, a Hasdeo-Arand forest is a natural gift to the state. When coal was found in nearby fields, mining of coal have become extended to the neighbouring forests also. The NGT has cancelled the plan for mining coal blocks. In November 2016, the Kolkata bench of NGT banned all solid waste and noise pollution in Sunderbans in order to protect wild life. It had also banned all kinds of construction activities in that eco-sensitive region. Illegal sand mining on the banks of the river Yamuna, Garbage dumping in West Delhi, Stubble burning in Fatehpur, Release of fly ash from power plant in Faridabad, and other industrial pollutions (air, water, solid waste disposals) are some of the few cases pending for the NGT's direction.

An environment is a clean and pollutant-free environment only if it constitutes people, things and matter what it is supposed to have. Otherwise, it is sure that damage is caused to the environment. A liquor shop cannot be allowed to run near schools and worshipping places like temple. A noisy, polluting factory cannot be allowed to run in residential areas. In Kanpur, construction material meant for Railways was piled up on the roadside for many days near a nursing home. By swift action by the Municipal Commissioner, the NGT took action on the contractors who irresponsibly used land that does not come under Railways.

The NGT has been credited for its landmark judgments for upholding environmental conservation. In the case of illegal construction alongside Goan costal regulation zone by a foreigner Betta Alwarez, the tribunal has cleared the issue by the order for demolishing the constructions. Over a lakh tonnes of raw garbage been untreated and piled up every day alongside the city outskirts in India. The tribunal directed the state and the centre to take necessary steps to remove the garbage and use them for building renewable energy resources.

Alaknanda Hydro Power Co. Ltd in Uttarkhand was asked to pay for damages caused by flooding of river which caused mass destruction of lives and property in the neighboring residential areas. Due to the untimely opening of reservoir gates during heavy rains, all the much and soil got carried to the villages. M.V. Rak was sinking with a load of coal, fuel oil and diesel close to the coast of South Mumbai causing a thick film of oil formed on the surface of the sea and large scale damage was caused to mangroves and marine eco system. Sinking of the ship was due to negligence and diligence of flouting the principles of pre-voyage. Case against the grant of environmental clearance given to a 6000-crore rupee hydro project in a bird sanctuary in Arunachal Pradesh was also cleared by the tribunal.

For many, nature is God. Nature too shows its reactions when disturbed. The growing damage to the ozone layer on the Antartic, the recent calamities of Tsunami and cyclones such as Katrina, Oki, Thane, Gaja and Nisha etc., are the warning signs of nature's vengeance at its increasing exploitation and environmental degradation. Landslides and volcanic eruptions are becoming frequent as global climatic conditions become unpredictable.

Health impact

Human health in its broadest sense depends on the access to a healthy environment for physical, mental and spiritual well-being. Frequent changes in climatic conditions and environmental pollution cause many diseases. Traditional diseases such as Malaria and viral fever have not yet been fully eradicated. Impure drinking water and unhygienic living conditions in urban areas are found to be the foremost source of health disorders. Nevertheless, occupation-related ailments, stress-related disorders and psychological mayhem are the outcomes of a spoilt environment. The current outbreak of Covid-19 virus is the best example for showcasing our pitiable environment in which we live and the poor health what we have with no immunity and nutrition.

The concepts of inter-dependency, shared planet, global citizenship are not just restricted to environmental issues alone. They apply equally to the shared and inter-linked responsibilities of environmental protection and human development. Problems are complex and the choices are increasingly becoming difficult. But, solution is just one. It is sustainable development. Bright future can only be achieved with a better understanding of our common concerns and shared responsibilities.

Gandhian- environmental movements

Gandhian non-violence is accepted by different environmental movements as a vital principle. Most of these movements lay claim to the Gandhian values of ecological prudence and frugality and to the Gandhian model of decentralized democracy and Village Swaraj. Many thinkers considered the Indian environmental movements like Chipko movement, Narmada Bachao Andolan (NBA) etc. as the living example of Gandhian Environmentalism and they consider Gandhi as a "man with deep ecological view of life, a view much too deep even for deep ecology." It was in Chipko movement that

Satyagraha was initially used as an effective technique to fight against environmental injustice. The Forest Satyagrahas of 1930's were a result of the Forest Act of 1927 which denied the people access to biomass for survival while increasing biomass production for industrial and commercial growth. The key agenda of the Chipko movement was that carrying forward the "vision of Gandhi's mobilization for a new society, where neither man nor nature is exploited and destroyed, which was the civilizational response to a threat to human survival."

Environmental movements in India used Satyagraha as the moral equivalent of war. Forest Satyagraha was first used effectively in Chipko movement to protest against deforestation. Gandhian techniques like *padayatras* were conducted to save nature. Conflict resolution techniques based on non-violence and self sacrifice were used by environmental activists like Chandi Prasad Bhatt, Baba Amte, Sunderlal Bahuguna, Medha Patker and others.

Gandhian Economy and Society

Over the last two decades, Indian villages have witnessed a series of development through various policies and promotional efforts from the government in the name of economic reforms. Private industries, corporate offices, educational institutions and research centres have cropped up in remote villages. Today, villages have access to satellite communication, wireless, Internet technologies, world-class schools, colleges, roads, transportation and educational facilities besides playing an important role in hosting their large vacant lands for setting up of multi-national companies and factories. Do all these constitute a localized economy what Gandhi had dreamed? Definitely not.

The localized economy what villages see today has been alarming and threatening to its very own existence. Village developments happen at the cost of arable lands, human values and inherent values the villages possess.

One may not immediately notice the serious damage that has been caused at the social level due to these economic activities and restructuring of villages. Not that this apprehension be discussed in the perception of westernization factor that has involved in these economic developments but the alterations occurred in the inherent social structure, values and belief existing in the society. Critical analysts and activists, pointing at the gradual declining of ethical values and social principles, are more bothered about the impact of economic activities on the conventional morality of the people.

The country will have to choose, and sooner the choice is made the better, between two economic policies viz. the conception of the welfare state as developed in the west, and the conception of economic life as reflected in Gandhiji's ideas. It is possible that to some extent the former can be modified by the influence of the latter. But it is obvious that the approaches of the two are entirely different and cannot be easily reconciled.

This universal urge for a higher and higher standard of living is the primary cause of the increasing danger of environmental disasters. The then U. N. Secretary-General had said in his report to it in 1969 : *"For the first time in the history of humankind, there is arising a crisis of worldwide proportion involving developed and developing countries alike - the crisis of human environment."* He attributed it to the explosive growth in populations, the poor integration of a powerful and efficient technology with environmental requirements, the deterioration of agricultural lands, the unplanned extension of urban areas, the decrease of available space and the growing danger of extinction of many forms of animal and plant life. It is increasingly apparent, he said, that if the current trend continues, the future of life on earth could be endangered.

Summary

Modern industrial development catering to economic growth and prosperity on one hand has contributed much of pollution and infrastructural changes causing damage to the ecosystem on the other. Technologies and manufacturing processes ushering to facilitate such development must first be scrutinized in order to sustain pollution-free environment. Just like the human factor is of supreme value in development, environmental factor is salient consideration in all our developmental activities. Keeping up the good environment and nature conservation is our moral duty.

Our industries are just a good servant but a bad master as we would realize that the widening of morality gap between developing technology and the state of human environment is highly dangerous. We cannot forecast the after-effects of certain development projects as it requires long period to do assess their impacts. In order to conserve the natural resources, our surroundings and our livelihood it is important to check the degree of moral forces plying in the industrial development.

India faces unprecedented concern over rising energy prices and their impact on our economic competitiveness and national security in an unstable world. Global climate change has the potential to dramatically alter the world environment. In addition, the relentless pressures of nationwide urbanization, manufacturing and population growth demand a renewed commitment to clean energy and environmental solutions.

The Environmental Impact Assessment and National Green Tribunal are just the policies what government might use to control environmental damages but it is for the entire nation, from villages to cities, from an individual to industrial groups, to have awareness about ecological preservation and sustainable development. Gandhi's nonviolence and movements based on his principles keep us learn the lessons in environment and must be one of the key drivers of India's economic growth. The challenges in the areas of sustainable management of natural resources, controlling of pollution and the right use of technologies need to be addressed through effective solutions and optimized processes.

"We cannot have ecological movement designed to prevent violence against nature, unless the principles of non-violence become central to the ethics of human culture" - Mahatma Gandhi

Covid-19

Covid-19 Corona virus has indeed invaded the whole world with its inexorable infection and the pandemic has taken the lives of millions of people off the track of normal business. Corona pandemic, started early in the month of January 2020, has been a worst disaster the world had seen after the two great World Wars. Whilst the wars had torn away the nations' growth and prosperity turning the geo-political nature of the world, this pandemic has had thwarted the routine life of people, socially, economically and politically.

This topic at large compares the state of humanity during the Covid-19 crisis from a Gandhian perspective. It elicits the socio-political environment that underwent drastic changes forcing the governments to go for complete lockdown on the normal course of life. The effects of Covid-19 in day-to-day regulars in education, science and technology are aptly discussed. It also ponders over how the world was running in terms of health, life and death during the pre-Corona days with the help of statistical figures collected as a sample. The final part of the topic examines the new normal that created opportunities for remote working in companies and its consequences in post-Covid environment.

Humanity Vs. Modern Science

In a war between humanity and natural calamity, it is the calamity that swallows the human lives forcing the whole mankind into a state of despair leaving all of us to continue our lives with a little bit of hope and faith for sustaining on this planet. In a war between Gandhian nonviolence and inventions and discoveries made by science and technology, we see the latter surpasses everything in the world as more and more of our lives continue to depend on tools and machines.

Covid-19, whether it is a natural calamity or human discovery, to this day it has outdone all our human gestures and compassion hitherto shown towards any disastrous, untoward, fateful happening in the world. The norms set to escape from the infection viz., keeping the social distance, washing hands, and wearing masks etc. have made for one time man's intellect inadequate. One might wonder, to what extent we don't know, how this kind of pandemic would keep our hands tied and hearts bleeding for the affected and deceased. For a layman, there exists really no human factor to save him and the fellow beings except for sure, to run for seeking the help from medical science and technology. People were already running towards modern science and technologies in the form of profession, or career or even as an independent species for survival.

Gandhian dictum of nonviolence and truth has always been challenged by the so-called non-believers who incessantly claim to traverse through the path of science and technology, enjoying the modernity and amenities provided by its inventions and discoveries, and testing all the time the powers of nonviolence and truth. Ironically, the world still runs smoothly and harmoniously because of the believers of those Gandhian values, but not the tech-trends. If 90% of the people goes behind science and technology, the remaining are left behind. The rest 10% prefer to stay behind despite all the enjoyments and amenities offered by S & T.

Assuming that Covid-19 is an artificial, human-made virus escaped from laboratories of Wuhan, China, those believers of science and technology would still celebrate that their faith had won in the race between science and humanity. For them, it is another milestone in an era of next generation of science and technology. If man-made pandemic is a breakthrough event in the history of modern science, inventing cure and inoculation is construed as another historic moment. What is ridiculing here is that the believers of Gandhian dictum of nonviolence and humanity-lovers would still prefer to stay in the remaining 10% of the population. The reason being that the trust and hope they had on the moral factor would slow down and bring the catastrophic modern science to a halt. They are hoping for a stage where developments beyond human wants would come into a saturation level. The 10% believe that all scientific developments do have a saturation point where even a single step further would damage the whole human kind that included environment and society first, and subsequently affecting the economy and other areas.

Assuming that Covid-19 is a natural born viral pandemic, lovers of modernity and other technocrats surely have won by arguing that there arisen a need for controlling the virus and finding a remedy. On the other hand, peace lovers and humanitarians argue that their beliefs are still good enough to lead a life amid such crisis. As Gandhi told, *"Simplicity is the essence of universality"*, the whole world hitherto running like a wild machine had come to a near still with the reduced work and the use of automobiles, machinery and tools.

Gandhian dictum of peace, nonviolence and humanity must be construed as a permanent cure for the life on the planet even though man is destined to seek towards using all his brains and nerves to advance in science and technology. The search for truth along the lines of modern science might yield temporary results but on the face of disastrous events there still needs an element of sympathy and humanity. The bad side of science shall not be dealt with science alone as it requires good men to work and good hearts to heal the injury caused by science. This pandemic has not given us a chance to fully exhibit the compassion towards the victims as it was a scientific blunder targeted towards killing millions of people.

Inoculation drive

U.K, U.S. India, China and Russia are the forerunning countries searching for a vaccine even as leading pharmaceutical companies claim that research is on to find the one. Pfizer-Biontech announced that their vaccine is ready during the first week of December 2020. The U.S also planned to launch the new vaccine in mid-December the same year. Vaccines such as Remedesivir, Covishield, Covaxin, Hydroxy-ChloroQuine are deployed in the medicine market to contain the pandemic.

The spread of the pandemic does not seem to be controlled by measures like face mask, hand sanitizers and social distancing. Every day, thousands of new cases are reported while hundreds die out of this deadly virus. Until mid-December 2020, as many as 15 crores have undergone 'Covid Test' in India, one of the largest in the world.

This pandemic had run through two to three ascends in a span of eight months with smaller periods of downward trend in parts of the world. But in India, it is steadily on the upward drift with a slower pace. Native medicines and herbal tonics are found to be preventive and curing at the symptomatic stages of the infection. Siddha medicines, Yoga practices and other hygienic measures are sufficient enough to escape from Covid-19 besides following the guidelines instructed by the medical agencies.

At the start of the pandemic, the world of hospitals, clinics and health centres had seen an unexpected fall in their line of business as they had to shut their services with no precise treatment available. Even so, some private hospitals admitted patients by charging exorbitant prices for a fortnight's stay with indigenous healing techniques. Vaccines like Remedesivir are charged ten times higher than actual price per dose as the demand grows more aggressively as months passed by.

Nevertheless, cure for the poor is at risk. For the deprived and low-income class people, it does not really matter whether the cure or vaccine is found for the Covid-19. They go with the government hospitals and government-run Covid special centers where they stay for months to wait for check-up and testing. Isolation wards and Intensive Care Units are for those who shell out money. It is also obvious that the new vaccinations invented are not for the poor unless it is distributed for free by the state-run hospitals and health centres.

All the cures and vaccination happens to be available only for a smaller fraction of people affected. It would take another three to five years to streamline the vaccination process throughout. India's economic condition and number of cases to be treated do not seem to make it easier to carry out this massive, pricey vaccination process. Statistics show that the U.S. and India equaled in number of vaccines applied but the population of two countries varies by a margin of more than fifty billions.

Societal sins

While speaking to an official of an electric crematorium in the city, I came to know about certain positive effects of the lockdowns imposed all over. "On an average, there were three hundred dead bodies that arrive usually for cremation for a month. During the first lockdown period from 25th March to 5th April in the year 2020, there were only hundred and twenty bodies have come..." he retorted. It is felt heartening to know that accidental deaths too have had come down significantly, due to less traffic. Also, it is reported that suicidal deaths have also had come to an almost nil. Pondering upon these stats, one could understand that clear roads with very little people or no traffic had yielded such lower mortality rates.

Even as people live at homes, most of the times together as family, suicidal instincts also have been reduced. Depression and inferior thoughts have gone away when people communicate each other, of course, with some social distance. Another reason could be the "evenness" or equality in remaining isolated. While everyone of us remain isolated, there arises no separate instinct or feeling of desolate or emptiness, which force people to commit suicide. Thus altogether, mortality rate has come down to almost 10%.

It is interesting to note that in a situation of many hospitals being shut down, rate of death is diminishing. How could it be possible? Aren't the people suffering various diseases and ailments other than Corona need to get hospitalized, treated successfully or fatally?

It is very difficult for one to understand this reversing trend of our lives. There are lots of untold, unexplored truths hiding behind this trend. It may end up sooner or later as we begin to realize that our beliefs becoming deceptive. And, this kind of exploration of our own experiences can be done only during such lockdown period. It requires panoramic research over all aspects of life that include medical science, social setup and laws. People do deserve to know such factual truths hidden in their life.

By staying at home, death parts away with us. This is one of the biggest changes the lockdown has brought to us. You are not going to be knocked down by a speeding vehicle or to acquire a dreadful disease as you are completely isolated from rest of the crowd.. For the same reason, out-patient wards in hospitals are also kept closed; Emergency admissions are not really as urgent as you believed. Diseases have been reduced. There are no sudden heart-attacks, brain hemorrhage, high blood pressure or any serious threat to your life. The whole of the world of health and medicine is directed towards the know-hows of Covid-19 virus and its effects.

How could it all be so transforming like this? No complaints. No treatments. In this Corona infectious times, number of deaths caused by other ailments has been reduced considerably. In-patients staying in the hospital wards are seeing improvements in their health. Only the older patients who had serious ailments in their vital organs succumb to illness. Corona has revolutionized the scenario to what even social activists or leaders fail to do.

All these magical changes arouse an interesting question now. Did Corona wipe out all other viruses? Or, was it all immoral economy of the hospital business? Having witnessed massive corporatization of our culture and lifestyle, even a small ailment such as cough and cold got colossal importance these days forcing us to visit a clinic. It also created a culture of relying on hospitals and clinics on a regular basis. Medical and pharmacy industries began to profiteer and flourish on the same grounds.

Above all, there is a beautiful change in people's normal life. Everyone is eating home-cooked food. Junk food, packed food and road-side snacks and chats have been banished. Our body metabolism is getting tuned to live in a nature-oriented lifestyle. Half the diseases might go away whilst we lead a simple life. No transportation; so, no accidents; No thefts or burglary; No genocide; No spoiled relations;

Corona, the mighty king might bring more such good changes. Let us face the future with a difference, with lots of hope! One shall not feel victimized during this lockdown period. This is the time when your positive energy comes into work. In Maharashtra, a couple dug a well not wasting their precious time. In Rajasthan, a school gets repainted by the workers who stayed there for quarantine. Online courses and Internet based work is in full swing in many parts of the world. All these constructive work may not bring their life back. But their working spirit and positive attitude seems to be up right and is on and on.

Remote Work

In India, work from home is sparsely adopted. Only a few high-tech companies and white collar jobs are working remotely. With the available Internet and Wi-Fi infrastructure, essential tasks of a day are accomplished. The staff and a few front-line workers are provided with smart phones and tools to complete their day-to-day routines. Nevertheless, it would not suffice to keep the run of the mill as busy as pre-Covid-19 days.

Lockdown has literally closed all production, logistics and team work. Remote work has given a portion of the crew in a factory a chance to try it out; It is noted that it is a new experience and strategic advantage what the management perceive for the future of the office. Remote work without commuting, in-person meetings and collaboration give them a chance to strategise certain operations to be carried out in future, completely in a new way. New plans, new schedules, new designs of work are being developed suitably to fit the new remote work situation. Yes, the change is inevitable.

Even as working from remote offers the companies a new dimension of management, staff and the workers still feel the missing human factor. Many people happily pursued the remote work initially have slowly begun to miss the human nuances in the work culture. Those who cheered the convenience, freedom and togetherness with family have started feeling that the work at office has lot more to offer socially. However, in the U.S. companies like National Insurance want to make it a permanent modality.

The New York Times attributed certain benefits of running office at home: shorter commutes, increased productivity, lower risk of contagion and savings on rentals and transportation.

Covid-19 has contributed to the beginning of remote work from where it ended. It sets off the biggest domain in the office space and work culture what the companies are still pondering upon. And, remote work could emerge as a new phenomenon in future diversifying the way we organize work and workmen.

The gap between the rich and poor

Divide between the rich and poor is increasingly widening these days. The gap between the private and government ownerships are also shrinking. All the efforts and theories suggested by economists and politicians are proven fatal as the world is under the grip of recession caused by man-made disasters and wrong policies.

Riches are making use of private services and privately-owned facilities as the poor are seeking for the support from government and states for their welfare needs. Privatization and disowning of various institutions and public sector industries have made people pay more for acquiring their service, (during the last decade, at least). The riches and the private entities have departed themselves from their dependency towards government except that taxation and regulations to follow for carrying out their operations. Governments are running towards extending their wholehearted help for corporate funding and privatization options, as it would hope to get the returns in the form of customs and taxes.

At any time of crisis, political or economic, poor people are left on the rampage symbolized by unemployment, inflation, price-rise and curbs on benefits. Take for instance, the Covid-19 crisis. The riches are immunized, treated in private clinics and hospitals as they are willing to pay for the medical services being offered to them. Not all the services, or similar kind of medical services, are offered to the poor, who go to government hospitals and Covid centers for their treatment. The poor pay less and get back lesser amount of services. The riches pay more, get benefited a lot.

Unemployment and diminished buying power of the poor people have put themselves vary far away from the riches. All the infrastructure, developments and progress seen in the past decade stand simply as a relics and residues of the poor's' hard work and the rich's money. The falling economy has literally put us a few decades behind as the nation and the world still have to find out new ways to keep it at expected levels what the scientists and economists promised a few years ago.

Trillion dollar economy…Sustainable Development Goals… Balanced global economies (oil, gold markets) have all become a day dream! Technological advancements, craze for cars and bikes, liberal lifestyle – all these have only facilitated the economy that pocketed the riches until a couple of years ago. Now the whole human race is diverted towards the problem of health and survival bringing an end to our thought of rapid economic development and next-level living style.

Back again, riches are rich. Poor are poorer. Limitations and restrictions on this Covid-19 situation have not brought equity or balance of life for all. Instead, the gap widens further. Lockdowns and remote work favours more to the riches, but not the poor. Oxygen crisis and shortage of vaccines are only for the poor, not for the riches. When Oxygen was not entirely available, it was a test for all. Once the production and procurement of medical oxygen mounts, the same is not readily accessible for the poor alone.

Riches are working and waiting for becoming richer. Private hospitals and clinics have thousands of beds vacant and could be filled only with rich patients. In the case of vaccines and oxygen cylinders, the states continue to beg the centre for them at free of cost. Public canteens and food centres are established by a group of poorer people to cater to the food requirements of the poor. Riches are confined at homes either following the lockdown rules or working remotely to become rich.

Thus so far, even nature divides the rich and the poor so dreadfully. Man proposes; God disposes!

Ruined Education

With the rise in Covid-19 pandemic situation all across the country, it is disheartening to know that the next wave of Corona virus is about to target kids and children which would be a devastating epoch in the middle of our year long fight against the virus.

Schools shut… Colleges and universities closed… For more than a year, primary and higher education has been severely affected due to this pandemic. What is worse in the situation is that the authorities could not weigh exactly the pandemic situation and its trends as they could not come up with concrete plans and guidelines to keep the children relaxed and hassle-free.

Even though the governments trying to guide the children and parents regularly about the start of the schools, conducting exams, admitting them in new courses, the corona pandemic has never allowed them so far to gauge the trending of the pandemic. Not a clear road-map could be drawn out as far as the future of education is concerned.

Some schools conduct online classes; some others conduct online exams; and few other schools ask students to attend in-person classes by providing safety measures. Yet the Indian government has categorically announced that it doesn't want to play with the life of students.

Entrance exams and graduation exams in colleges and universities are very important to select candidates based on merit and quality of skills. Public exams conducted for 10th and 12th standard students are very important for seeking admission in colleges and universities. Millions of students across the country need to write these exams on time to pursue their education and career seamlessly. Teacher-Student direct communication and interactive classes are required to provide education to children at all levels.

But these things did not happen. Covid waves continue to perturb our education system. Our children continue to suffer, fear about their education which is adding more stress to parents as well. Online classes do not suffice enough to impart valuable training and quality education. Without exams, evaluation and performance becomes impossibility.

All we need now is a new model of education to provide quality education and adequate knowledge to the children without disturbing their mindset and psyche. We need a new model that caters knowledge and skills to children without bothering their mental health and adding stress and strain. India is proposing an optimized model for virtual learning to all children, of from primary to higher education. With reduced syllabi, simplified procedures for examinations, firm decisions on the future course of school education, children could be freed from stress, fear and uncertainties. We need a single window system to protect our children from rising Covid infections. That new model must include a mandatory vaccination for children below 18 years. That new model needs to be done at the earliest.

Science and Technology

Science and Technology rules the world! Is it in the hands of the right people? This is the biggest question the 21st century faces today as it is marked by the supremacy of computers and Internet, Smart phones and electronic gadgets for its extravaganza, yet struggling to come out of the jinx and pain they have caused.

Technology has taken people to the newer ways of life. Almost all walks of life is powered and supplemented by technological inventions. The rapid technocracy has not only enabled the humans to perform their functions efficiently and fast, it also took some shortcomings as well.

Covid-19 that was borne in the province of Wuhan, China is the best example for science and technology best misused. It thwarted the whole world in to debris of distrust, sickness, fatality and more significantly the lifestyle what the new century had created in the early 2000s.

Misuse of science and technology reverses the whole purpose of what it meant to be. The economic growth, intellectual progress, human welfare and delight – all these have had vanished if any of the technologies go wrong.

Think about technologies changing lives in a better way on the one side; On the other, we have the same expertise and skills going in vain. A steep growth we had seen with the use of inventions and innovations have seen a sudden fall. A wrong hand expertise and a notorious leadership would take us no where even if we continue to strive and thrive with the help of technologies.

The world of medicine and immunization has continued to discover newer remedies for growing pain we suffer due to Covid-19. Billions of people exchange their ideas and experiences just in a fraction of second using the Internet. Crisis management and disaster management teams continue to develop new models of working to cope up with the situations. With pandemic and subsequent lockdowns widens the gap between the people, the world is still shrinking as we are up-to-date in learning what is going on in our planet.

All such developments bring hope and faith in our own brains. We as a human-kind trust our knowledge and capacity to rule the world despite all catastrophes.

But, we must remember that man-made catastrophes are an outcome of the same intellect which delivered compassion to our problems. It is the same human brain that develop tools to usher our livelihood has destructed our lives as well.

Let the Science and Technology continue to rule the world. Let the superfast planes and trains come into our daily hood. Let the human race inhabit the extra-terrestrial planets. Let robots and drones live with us as a family. Let all these maintains and control all of our activities and feelings too.

Yet there needs a benevolent human behind every machinery; to check out these tools and gadgets running the world wisely, humanly. Let them all stay with good hands to serve good to the humanity.

Lets' not see another scientist spreading virus; Lets' not see a nation raging war against another. Lets' not see a human destroying another human; Lets' not allow drones dropping bombs.

Let the Science and Technology heals the virtues, not cherish the sins. Let our inventions alleviate our problems, not in- humanize us.

The new normal

What Gandhi would do if he happens to witness mass killings and inhuman treatments meted out in hospitals and other public places due to Covid-19 like pandemic?

The world has gone out of gears when the Covid-19 virus broke out last year wielding many restrictions and turning the routine work into a mess. Millions affected by the virus couldn't get their health checked and treated as the cure was not yet discovered. But after a few months, when vaccines made available, the world has just realized how massive the whole exercise was to produce, distribute, vaccinate billions of people amid the never ending spread of the pandemic. With economic activities coming to a halt, trade and commerce falling to a new low, it was not that difficult for the entire world to feel the bite of the nasty recessive tiger. Financial crunches, non-availability of the essential commodities, no income – all augmented the pressure exercised by the physical restrictions like wearing masks, maintaining social distancing, no outing, sanitizing bodily things.

Pressure from two extreme ends, physical isolation and inactive life-style, forced the world to create, develop new norms to lead a new life. Be it professional, public or private routines and practices, it required everywhere a new normal that comprised a limited set of resources, access to those resources and consuming selective resources in order to meet the demands of everyone.

At least for now, for one time in the history of the world, mankind has yielded to the sustainable requirements for the sake of his fellow mankind. For decades, the world is trying to find ways to lead a sustainable life, at least in theory, shifting its focus towards the need for renewable energy, forestation, reducing pollution, cut down global warming and climate changing effects etc. Gandhi's model of life is all about simplicity, fulfilling the basic needs of the society, embracing the nature and normal tendencies of human kind. In a way, the pandemic has largely strained whole of the world to such an environment with the advent of new norms.

For Gandhi, it wouldn't be a different idea at all for he firmly chose to live a traditional village life what the new norms preaches us today. Economics says, "when the demand is more, supply is less." This very principle itself is shattered by the conditions set by the pandemic. We face shortages of everything we need. But it is not always economics or economic development! Human relations and moral standings needed to live as a society is what more important for Gandhi.

The new norms have derailed, not to blame anyone, the ethical part of our lives. Hearing news about someone dying every hour is not shocking news anymore! Because, it has become habitual to lose someone every other day even whilst new normal is in practice. With pollution drastically reduced to unprecedented levels, we still need oxygen for medical purposes. Alas, we do not have it in suffice. After few deaths, we buy, produce, and import oxygen in this new normal. Vaccinations - a solace to the entire menace. But, we could not do it for all. All we can do is what the new normal allows us to do.

This pandemic has thrashed us into dust. It comes as a curse to the neglect, greed and inhumanity we have nurtured for centuries. The new normal talks about professional life with restrictions and social conditions. It shows us how to earn and spend money, how to clean and be hygienic, how to listen to government orders, how to follow rules.

The new normal suffices enough to tackle the changed environment due to Covid-19 pandemic. Nevertheless it is not the end. It is not the destiny. We are going to return to normal. And, what is that normal? Hopefully, Gandhi would bring about that REAL, NEW NORMAL! Gandhian way of living is the best bet for changing times of crises.

People against Vaccination

While India is surpassing a record billion Covid vaccinations across the country, many countries are still facing the struggle in making their vaccine mandate difficult and hesitant. As people come to streets protesting the vaccine mandate posed by the governments in countries like U.S., U.K., Australia, Germany and other

European countries, what is occurring to my thought is really displeasing and deplorable to some extent.

What is the truth behind these vaccine mandates marked by protests by thousands of people?

As almost six hundred thousand people already dies due to Covid in the U.S., people are still skeptical to go for government sponsored Covid tests, vaccines and procedures as they continue to claim that their freedom is largely impounded by the authorities. Wearing masks, keeping a social distance and other guidelines suggested by the medical authorities are safely ignored by such protestors. Many of them believe that the Covid pandemic itself is a government sponsored scheme.

People's disappointment and dejected mindset may be true or reasonable enough to demand more serious, responsible action by the governments; but it looks like protestors are motivated by some unknown beliefs, distrust and obstinate forces aimed at thwarting the world which is already in to a wreckage by the infliction of pandemic into a state of chaos and delusion.

What is more to come? This pandemic kick started in March 2020 has swept the whole world by its dreadful panic amongst the scientists and medical world besides killing millions of people is yet to be curtained and discovered. True. After all, our doctors and scientists have not seen such a 'touch-me-not' kind of virus which had killed for at least thousand doctors worldwide.

Many business houses and workplaces do not allow their workmen and customers not vaccinated. Even as many unvaccinated people coming out freely out on the roads, it is not sure for them if they had protected themselves against the Covid. It is just an act of both fearlessness and resistance from the part of protestors.

On the contrary, a portion of my insight wants to congratulate those protestors who not only defied the rules and guidelines set by the government, but for challenging the Covid itself. For them, it is an outright displeasure and disregard for the entire situation developed over this pandemic. For them, Covid-19 is nothing but a virus spread by Chinese laboratory in 2019. For them, Covid is another reckless scheme, vaccination, a mandate by the greedy governments.

While countries speaking high of democracy and people's power take vaccination a practical solution to escape from the clutches of Covid-19, only the powerful nations are slipping towards the uncertainty over the measures, digging further and further to find out more and more on this pandemic. They discovered Covid variants; vaccines of various perfection levels, new model for schooling, Work from Home culture in corporate, a fresh look out from municipal corporations, and finally a sect of protestors who still do not believe that Covid a virus.

Covid Variants

With more than a year spent on study and analysis in developing cures and vaccines for Covid-19, scientists worldwide have shown an whopping rate of success and stability over the deadly virus. Even as many criticisms prevailed over the findings and implementation process of vaccination along with much larger politicization of vaccine supplies and mandates, countries have successfully sailing through the fateful phenomenon called pandemic.

It was in December 2019 when Corona was first discovered and leaked in the Wuhan laboratories of China that sparkled a huge pandemic situation across the world.

The panic and disorder caused by the pandemic was no less than any other disastrous natural calamity as the governments have been trying to contain it for months, looking for a suitable model to cope up with the situation. Cleanliness tasks and controlling measures as suggested by the concerned authorities have come as a consolation amid suspicions and denigrating feedbacks. With the advent of vaccines made available a year ago, vaccination has been projected as a sole remedy cum preventive measure to tackle the Covid infections.

But, studies continue to inform us that exceptional cases are far too safe from any kind of measures such as quarantine, vaccination or medication.

Things got complicated when the first case of a variant of Covid, named 'Delta +' was detected. Delta variants too was spreading like its predecessor, but with added symptoms.. Unlike Covid -19, Delta variants was scarce and was seen little scary as people have already been experienced with the effects of Covid-19. The question, How the SARS-COV-19 virus transformed into a variant? – is not yet convincingly answered! Scientists continue to offer half-truths relating to mutants and malformation theories.

By the end of 2021, another variant named "Omicron" was found in South Africa. It was found to be another mutant of Covid with milder symptomes but not lethal! More and more cases of Omicron is coming out now trying to outnumber the original Covid-19. Many European countries and American nation have witnessed third and fourth wave of Covid-19 besides finding the traces of Delta variants and newly found Omicron.

Adding to this gloom , scientists reiterated that much more lethal variants (Neo-Cov in 2022) are coming in the future! Considering the earlier predictions stating that this pandemic would hang about in another couple of years, efforts put on to curb the pandemic is way too small and weary, and direction-less.

Our greater concern is: Are these variants emerge out of aboriginal ways of mutation or another clandestine leakage operations carried out from undisclosed laboratories? If Wuhan labs got shut after its connection with the Covid-19 swell, from where these variants are developed, London, South Africa or America? And, why scientists around the world play with this Corona aspect of human lives as they could not come up with clear answer on how Covid-19 transform into variants?

Summary

Covid-19 pandemic has left a little for humanity to shine. No touch, no closeness, no hugs, no sharing and some times, even no compassion. It demonstrated the need for cleanliness, healthy habits and more importantly, consumerism- the volume of usage of day-to-day things without which we could not have lived our life in the recent decades. And for those who are not affected with Covid virus, it drove them to a kind of nostalgic life full of serenity, freshness, hale and hearty lifestyle amid growing uncertainties of the lives of affected ones.

The science behind Covid-19 has made us to realize the true potential of the science of nonviolence. The socio-political forces hitherto working with differences and inconsistencies have all come together to rise to the occasion for the uplift of the whole mankind from the death bed of malicious virus attack. If it was all that science is behind Covid-19, sure that we as humans would come out of this catastrophic failure. As Gandhi himself pointed out, "The word 'failure' has no place in the vocabulary of science."

The socio-political conditions that kept us on toes towards economic greediness and limitless wants have become pale and dormant during the period of this crisis. The pandemic period has restricted us to the lowest bounds in all aspects of life including food, health, education, work, sports etc., dimming the brighter sides of life.

It forces the man, machinery and money powers those ruling the world to look into another dimension of choices and limits within the same socio-political sphere. Thus so far, the world has begun to prepare a new normal for our future life on an experimental basis. The post-Covid environment, hopefully, would have a new, secured framework of things to meet any challenges in future.

Pricing and Inflation

Rising inflation is not a new phenomenon. It is a direct outcome of the ways the world was progressing for over a decade now with its globalized economy that has nurtured only a selected few to grow and prosper in extraordinary ways. Global market is owned by that few to cater to the needs and unjustified wants of the corporatized crowd who were mesmerized, induced by the strategies and lavish lifestyles preached by their bosses. Regrettably, the same is determining the economic state of the countries worldwide. Another lamentable face of this burlesque economic development activities is that it keeps the welfare of the people at bay despite being cautioned by Covid-19 pandemic which has thwarted everything what the world has developed hitherto, causing a lot of pain and suffering to people damaging the economy built over the years in the past.

Higher inflation rates are marked by higher prices of commodities, which would gradually bring down the buying power of the people. With services and service-oriented businesses propping up to support the global economy, it has become imperative to keep a vigil not only on the prices, but on the service-sector as well.

India's inflation has been consistently on the upward trend because of growing unemployment, rising prices of food and energy. Fuel imports and prices are continuously inconsistent during the last few years, which is seen as the main cause of the rise of prices. Middle classes and the poor had to pay a minimum 15% extra from their pockets for their day-to-day living.

The U.S., the largest economy in the world, is not an exception, either. It has seen a forty-year high of 8.5% inflation rate even as the issues of unemployment and liquidity were addressed adequately.

The International Monetary Fund publishes the World's Economic Outlook data book each year. In 2021, it puts India's inflation at 5.56%, the U.S at 7.12%, the U.K at 2.19%. Switzerland's inflation rate is 0.0% a nil change in the consumer prices whereas Japan, Sweden among a very few countries show deflation, a sign of decreasing prices. The countries Sri Lanka(inflation rate 5.16%), Bangladesh(5.5%), Pakistan(8.9%) and Sudan(194.6%) witnessed violence and agitation at its worst towards economic recession, driven by heavy prices of food, beverages, fuel that had ultimately disrupted other services leading to a change in political leadership.

A close examination on the reports of inflation and its effects in many countries, it has come to light that consumer prices are invariably soaring high because of business priorities and policies adopted by the governments. While pandemic conditions and the 'new normal' contributed towards change in lifestyles and in our priorities socially, businesses are prioritized and categorized, as well. Health services, eateries and food deliveries, electronic communications and media devices have undergone drastic changes, and the prices in these sectors soared high as demands were snowballing to irrepressible levels. It created a business environment that required a special care on the economy from the governments. But, it didn't happen.

Even as the U.S. government was working on the lost jobs, the fallen economy is not gaining ground. India is sustaining this downward trend with no major casualties. Selling of government owned industries, public enterprises adds to the exchequer. Millions of people shell out billions of rupees just on health care, which attracted a considerable volume of taxed amount, say Goods and

Services Act (GST). Government's plans to decentralize its finances and give the states more autonomy pay some benefits. Government sponsored liquor shops, medical centres and other online services give it a soothing boost to the economy.

However, a failing economy is not an issue of the government's exchequer. Rupee value continues to fall even as the U.S. is crying for stabilizing its economy. India's imports and exports suffer even while the relationship is at its best with the major trading countries. Adding to the exchequer in the form of taxes need to be returned to the taxpayers through schemes that build their economies, rather than siphoning more taxes for the infrastructure or for their education, health or welfare services. Where is all the money going? A selected few gets the contract from the government for building infrastructure, roads and other services. Even public welfare schemes are subcontracted to only those who pay bribes and who are influential in politics.

Such disparities and discrimination would cause inflationary conditions, as equities will not reach everyone's pockets. Moreover, those who are deprived may get into things that would possibly spoil economic conditions. Lots of work and contracts go into the wrong hands making things worse, causing damage and ruining the economy. For instance, Digital India produces nothing productive or economically gainful, but offers services that incur costs on selective machinery.

Vending machines… Access doors… Shopping centres… Toll roads…all purchases of goods and services, even paid toilets in public places… All these need QR code; or, Gpay, Phonepay or Paytm like apps in your smart phones. And there are around 40% of the world population still not using such electronic services. They can't afford them is just another reason. A portion of people have sold or mortgaging smartphones for their day-to-day food. Digitization Is Humanity's Demise. The "Smartphonization" of Humanity. The QR Code is Everywhere.

Where did those hard-talking economists gone? Governments of the world is really in the soup at the clutches of inflation, these days. Not that it is due to pandemic or lockdowns, which initiated the inflation as many believe, but years before and after, people of the world paying 'heavy prices' almost for everything they buy. Russia-Ukraine war merely fuel the price rise, they know. But nobody knows what to do to contain this malicious daemon!

Oil Economy

The world of oil barons is desperately in need of a charter that spells out the equation for balancing the price and consumption of fossil fuel and alternative energy to stay in business in the coming years. After COP27, geared by the world leaders, climate activists and environmentalists, developed countries are into a paced mechanics of seeking solutions to cut carbon emissions and enhance renewed energy needs.

For Joe Biden the POTUS, it may be very optimistic to roll out thousands of electric cars on the roads of the U.S. What the U.S. is doing to promote battery-operated vehicles could be a line of control for fossil oil producing countries to sit and talk about their future. Of course, it involves the future of the U.S. as well when it comes to sustainability, availability and practical use of solar-powered or electric vehicles.

As far as the other nations, it is a complex, heterogeneous market yet to be explored. It may be far-sighted to place a price cap of $60 a barrel of crude to augment the green plans initiated by the European Union and G7 countries.. And Russia, the largest oil producer in Europe, rejecting the crude oil price cap could well be seen as its retaliatory standpoint besides rising doubts about its green policy.

The complex situation of Russia's invasion on Ukraine, crude price limits and growing demand for renewed energy-based vehicles has put the world to look for a new paradigm for balancing the disparities between the developed and the developing world.

For Russia, the price cap is a loss of revenue. Denouncing the cap would mean a pressure on the U.S. and the European Union oil market forcing a change of equation in oil consumption and pricing. This would indirectly affect the green-energy plans which has just been kicked off in many countries in the West.

Countries like India, China and Turkey are already enjoying the discounted price on Russia's crude. Electric cars and charging stations are making a big way in these countries even as they need to meet the expected carbon emission levels by 2050. However it is not the only reason for the emergence of electric vehicles. Growing number of salaried consumers opt for e-vehicles as they begin to feel that the fuel price is exorbitant and out of their monthly budget.

On a wider basis, the 'crude war' over the supply and pricing of fuel between the oil producing countries and buying countries has literally diluted the onus on the 'green agenda for reduction of global warming' and CO2 emission level targets in developing countries. Even as electric cars are being rolled out as a measure for the upliftment of 'pollution-free, renewed energy', the ethos for a clean environment is still lacking.

Now the biggest question is: What will be the future of fossil-oil based vehicles? And, will the renewed energy goals be met? In India, 15-year old diesel run vehicles are already asked to leave the roads. Automobile companies like Tesla are investing and expanding new hubs for electric cars. Solar power is equally given a push. But what is missing is a clear correlative charter that speaks of economic, environmental aspects involved in these developments.

For instance, the $430 billion inflation reduction push has driven away many industries from the U.S. Even to tackle the inflation, countries need to check their manufacturing strategies in order to keep up with the sustainability goals. There comes the game of choice between fossil fuels and renewed energy which has a larger impact on economic growth of every country. It is essential for nations to keep their climate actions that include pollution control, carbon emission,global warming etc.,in sync with the anti-inflation plans and manufacturing capacity.

To put it simply, industries need to think about what to manufacture, automobile cars or electric cars? Governments need to think about renewed policies targeting the right industry for the benefit of environmental safety and sustainability. At the same time, both the private and public parties need to ensure the minimum prices and taxes to cut inflation rates.

A global charter for global economic development that covers all these aspects is the need of the hour. We we need a common, minimum charter that comprises all of these elements, their trends and future to obtain the sustainable results. That would guarantee smoother progress across the world ubiquitously.

Current standings as on 2022-23:

- Russia cuts oil production in view of $60 price cap by EU

- India supports Russia and doesn't want to reduce inland petrol/diesel price and is happy to pay less dollars for crude
- EU is happy to cut the Russia's rein over oil economy
- U.S. oil exports rising high as crude price matches with Russia's.

Persistent inflation, oil market and automobile manufacturing industries, and climate change actions to control global warming and pollution, clean atmosphere – all these are interconnected to each other. We can't just set right one of these to exploit the benefits of setting it right; other areas are equally pressing us to seek attention. Economy, Production and Consumption and innovative ways of green technologies need to be addressed with a collective, unison thought and approach. This article talks about why we need a common, minimum charter that comprises all of these elements, their trends and future to obtain the sustainable results.

RUSSIA-UKRAINE WAR

First, the world must '*remove the mind-set of the possible Third World War*' what the west is reckoning upon this unrelenting war between Russia and Ukraine. NATO and rest of the world support Ukraine and supply more and more weapons thinking that this would grow in to a big, big World War. It is just a miscalculation! To stop war between any two countries, internationalization of war must be stopped. Hope not for escalation of the Russia-Ukraine war beyond its boundaries.

Communist Hand

Communist governments in Russia and China have become greedier than ever before with their launch of war on Ukraine and Covid-19 pandemic respectively. And they talking about global issues like climate change, green technology and social health and welfare is just a flattering shake hand with the global communities.

In October 2022, Russia annexed four or more regions in the Ukraine territory and brought them under its control. Ukraine damaged the important railroad bridge between Russia and Crimea as a retaliation effort in its defence against Russia's aggression.

Those who fled Ukraine are still out in neighbouring countries and are not back; not in the near future. The fight between the military forces of Russia and armed people in the interiors of the East and Southeast continue to last with no ending in sight.

The reconciliation talks by Belarus, Poland and the U.S. backed NATO do not seem to change the 'Big Putin' of Russia to turn the tables. Russia, under Putin's regime, has put the nation at the top of the list of most dangerous countries. The U.N. warnings and sanctions from the U.S. and other nations have not shaken Putin's acquisition plan through aggression and attacks.

The oil and gas deals with Russia have affected global trade significantly. The trade barriers and restrictions have bitten even Russia's closest allies like China and India whereas it reversed the economic growth in the most relevant countries like SriLanka, Pakistan, and other Euro-Asian countries.

The democracies in the world see growth and prosperity by implementing globalizing policies, decentralization of assets and processes. Even the flattened economies thrived with the help of polarizing the powers of economy allowing the industries and finances to feed the failing parts of the economy. Governments worldwide are working towards decreased pressures on taxations, interest rates and freebies to ease out the inflation thus decelerating the effects of recession.

Russia, along with China, is the largest Communist regime in the world. They did take part in the globalization and liberalization of economies worldwide, deepening over the last two decades. Under Putin's rule, Russia's economy was challenging and competing. Yet, communist ways of development have their own pitfalls.

Centralized authority of power and accumulation of wealth at the centre of the federalism have gotten its toll in the form of Ukraine's effort in joining the NATO countries. It is like a cold war kind of scuffle inside between Russia and its 'child' countries like Poland, Ukraine, and Belarus. Until February 2022, relations between Russia and Ukraine were not that good as Ukraine is disproportionately divided as pro-Russian and anti-Russian sects.

Communist governments in both countries pay focus on acquiring wealth and resources leaving the people to make their choices on socio-political orientations. It allowed the lobbying of people to espouse western (European) culture, to thrive upon globalized economic outlets, and be void of ethnic Russian origins of lifestyle.

Political observers are still wary of the democratic, diplomatic ways of resolving the ongoing war between Russia and Ukraine. Quite obviously, a war should not be politicized. War is like at the tip of the iceberg-kind of condition that the concerned nations have built for years. Also, it is vivid that governments involved in the war are solely responsible for uprooting normalcy between the warring nations and the rest of the world.

However, one thing is noteworthy, here. It is because of Communism that the rulers of both the nations have gained overwhelming autocratic powers causing such destruction. People's voices have become feeble while the government authorities unanimously take decisions both on attacking strategies and for the reconciliatory moves, if any, if at all.

Communism has made the people run away from their own land for the cause of war and destruction. In democracies, such migration happens due to ethnic, racial or communal fights amongst the people themselves. In democracies, people's revolution would give a change in the game of conflict or war.

Communism has failed its people, at last, in Russia, Ukraine and to say it precisely the former Soviet Union as they have no other option except to battle, for longer and longer until they exhaust themselves. Only a state of exhaustion of forces, resources and what more, the desire and greed of the leaders involved – alone could stop the war.

Ukraine has everything that Ukrainians need but not for Putin's greed. While Covid-19 pandemic has paved the way for a 'new normal', the repercussions of the Russia-Ukraine war have created 'another new normal' in the global economy and politics. The U.N., NATO and other world organizations are working towards this 'another new normal' tackling the menace of this war and its implications. Nuclear threat from Russia is clearly driving the programmes in the world that was already grounded by the economic recession caused by oil trade.

Communist Russia, its allies including China have gained during the past globalization era. At a time when these nations proposed to return something useful to the world, China's hand in the pandemic and Russia's invasion of Ukraine is a moment of frustration to socialist, capitalist, democratic nations. Communism in these two nations has prompted them to plunder, accumulate and consolidate wealth in their governments exploiting the globalization plans to the fullest. It is not ending. In terms of Ukraine invasion, pandemic measures, and 'new normal', it continues endlessly. People are forced to adopt their massive plans meant to tackle manmade disasters and pay more on taxes and for the bills. Needless to mention the oppressive government policies are quite despotic enough to cart people running after pillars to corners to make things happen. None of the communist policies would improve the conditions prevailing today due to economic recession and inflation.

The Economics Nobel Laureate Abhiji Bannerjie once remarked, "all welfare economists are left-leaning economists". It may be true only for communism; communism alone flourishes economically through policies drafted by such economists, at the cost of paying heavy prices on people.

The greedy communist governments in Russia and China talking about global issues like climate change, green technology and social health and welfare is just a flattering shake hand with the global communities. But, pocketing millions of dollars for quenching its communist agenda negates the tenacity of these issues that are having a great impact on world peace and economic growth.

According to a global study by the climate scientists from Rutgers University, over 5 billion would die of hunger following a full-scale nuclear war between the U.S. and Russia.A team consisting of Alan Robock and Lili Xia, Department of Environmental Sciences, Rutgers University have calculated how much sun-blocking soot would enter the atmosphere from firestorms that would be ignited by the detonation of nuclear weapons. Based on calculated soot arising from six war scenarios, - five smaller India-Pakistan war and a large the U.S.- Russia war based on the quantum of each country's nuclear arsenal.

April 2023

With more than a year passed by now, Russia has not stopped its brutal war on Ukraine.

NATO and rest of the world support Ukraine and supply more and more weapons thinking that this would grow in to a big, big World War. It is just a miscalculation! Peace is a big question now.

Of course, the world is seriously in trouble now facing the war implications politically and economically. Trade restrictions on Fuel prices and supplies. Changing political equations that severe relationships, Economic instability in the third world due to shortage of supplies and monetary deficits, Covid pandemic situations and above all challenging Climatic changes.

While the Russia-Ukraine war does not see an end, world is busy mending on all these crucial issues that require attention on a day-to-day basis. Actually, nobody wants war. We have no time to rage war. We are more focused on sustainable development! This is our status-quo.

It does not mean that we are waiting for the Third World War, in a big way! After all, who wants war! The whole world is still fighting to come out of other ills like economic recession, Covid-19 and the like.

Russia is ready for talks with Ukraine, but not willing to leave the occupied regions. In G20 talks held in India, PM Narendra Modi said, "Todays' era is not of war!" The West applauded his notion politically, but must have a firm conviction to carry the same message to NATO, and ensure the withdrawal of arms supplies to Ukraine, and put an end to the devastating attacks on Ukraine. G20 talks on peace shall not go unheard or left-behind here in New Delhi.

The fate of lost territories need to be addressed diplomatically and by political means. People who flee from those regions shall have to return and exercise their democratic powers, which requires a small respite in the ongoing war. The fate of Ukraine is not limited to just destruction, but a way to build a sort of resilience.

Democracy bleeding

Ukraine is pleading the west for more weapons! For what? With over a million Ukrainians taken refuge in the neighboring countries including Russia, what the rest of the Ukrainians staying inland gotta do? Just fight with

Russian army and die? No democracy can tolerate or pardon what Zelenskyy is doing in Ukraine.

The war in Ukraine has left its people naive and insensible in terms of reacting to the attacks from Russia. With more than hundred days of Russia-Ukraine war already taking place in the Ukrainian soil, people of Ukraine have not learned lessons of being a legitimate citizen on their own.

More than a million of people, including women and children, have been migrated to the neighbouring countries accepting the dreadful fate of the war, losing the future and their belongings. To brief it further, they have actually lost a minutest sense of finding a more 'respectable' way of handling the war situation. May be, this could be the choice for those who do not want to leave the country, but to face the Russian attacks.

What the observers mean to divulge here in the Russia-Ukraine war situation is budding like an after-thought flashlight changing the entire clout over the future of the war. It is somewhat alarming when few of them say, 'it is better to die than to be enslaved as refugees' It sounds quite rational to think of no escaping from the Russian attacks, but to face it harder and die. For a Ukrainian, the situation portrayed by the rest of the world is misleading and discomforting. It is not actually the Ukraine's aspiration to become a NATO member or to secure a sovereign state independent of Russian control alone decides the crisis; when the war broke out, it becomes an issue of humanitarian crisis.

Observers feel that becoming a refugee might not be the right option to deal with. A 'Do or Die' kind of attitude is completely missing, not to mention the strategic methods to counter the attacks. Shortly, the world is running Ukraine today amid Russian attacks. The spirit of Ukraine and its citizens is completely lacking.

Then again, few other observers want the Ukrainians to deal the situation politically. Democratic upraises or emergence of alternative leadership might have happened if it were happened in some other country. No protests or disparate views on Zelenskyy are completely lacking. A change in leadership might bring some changes in the Russian perception over the differences between the two nations. Ukrainian citizens do believe in democratic ways of functioning; in these critical days of war, it lacks that spirit.

Instead, Ukrainian leadership is seeking for the help from the rest of world. European Union and the U.S.A. sent ammunition and weapons to Ukraine. Millions went out of the country as refugees living an enslave life along the borders begging for food and alms, and other basic amenities. Inland, a few thousands took to the arms fighting back, attacking Russian tanks and soldiers. A political, diplomatic solution is too farther to reach as the world watches helplessly facing the economic back-kicks arising out of this war.

Knowingly or unknowingly, the world has picked up the fears of World War III during the initial stages of Russia-Ukraine war. Perhaps the government and the people of Ukraine might have tagged along in that direction. War hunger nations do supply weapons and stimulate attacks further. Ukraine had listened to the world beyond a level of gratitude where everyone believed the war would end soon. Now, it has become sick. It is horrendous for the whole world to live with this war involving two nations.

Why would Ukraine want such an inept, clueless president? Why do not the people choose a competent person to deal with the crisis? Why not a president who could work with Russia peaceful plans and smoother transition to the common interests?

At the face of death, escapism or fighting back may be reckoned as a destiny. However, people's democracy and systemic changes might have been tried to save the sovereignty and dignity of the nation.

World War in Economics

World is seriously heading towards an economic war in top-gears that could ravage the countries hitherto running smoothly as far as economic growth is concerned. The aggression and cut-throat developments has turned over millions of dollars in certain sectors of business causing competitive spirit among the business tycoons around the world, and a sense of jealousy and greed driving them into unforeseen ventures and dirty games, as well.

With the Russian invasion in Ukraine unfolded instantaneously after the induction of 'new normal' set for handling post-pandemic conditions, business ventures and policies have taken a new shift in their direction towards lifting the economy. Gross Domestic Product, price indices of consumers, rural and urban harmony and shares have all plunged to a new low pushing the markets to rethink once again to exploit the situations developing due to the war. Even as the post-pandemic developments drive nations to sustain their economy, rising inflation and uncertain markets are steadily giving a thrust to a possibly slowed-down, recessive economy globally

Russia and China are well-known rivals to the west in the production of electronic goods, software and mobile apps business. Russia's crude oil has constituted almost 80% of the U.S. oil imports whereas the Chinese items are dominating half the market worldwide. Just a while after the Japanese occupation ceased to exist in the computer and electronic goods market, China and Russia have consistently shown their presence with their wide-range of products, apps and services. The U.S. dominated Internet of Things (IOT) is promptly seized by Chinese companies.

Now, the real war is happening amongst the top business tycoons in the world. The former co-founder of Microsoft and philanthropist Bill Gates has diversified himself into various bio-medical projects triggering a new level of competition to the existing players. His sponsorship to the scientific projects to kill mosquitoes and anti-Covid vaccines are just a few to name that had gone into controversies. The advent of electric cars by Tesla and the rise of Elon Musk to the top of the chart for the world's richest men have sparked a new fire in the race of production of cars across the world. The professional rivalry between Amazon's Jeff Bezos' satellite venture Project Kuiper and Elon Musk's SpaceX is not just about innovative business. It is about amassing billions from the pockets of people and provoking other billionaires to dive into similar such missions. The race for becoming the richest man in the world is vividly open even while the same is turning into an economic war between the companies.

With all these changes in the corporate ventures and large welfare schemes, the entire financial system is going to change very soon, economists predict. They also indicate that the mainstream media has categorically ignored these developments. The crucial meet at the United Nations Climate Change Conference (COP26) in 2021 in Glasgow, Scotland attracted powerful business leaders who committed to make this 'global transition' of economy.

Investigative journalist and noted economist Nomi Prins discovered a few startling findings that might cause the whole world to think twice while making any new investments. She says, "I have found evidence the elites are working together to 'transform' our economy into something we did not vote on... Did not ask for... And very few are prepared for." Click here for her interview.

The war in Ukraine has created a new space for this economic war involving not only rich individuals and elites, but the global institutions such as the International Monetary Fund (IMF), the World Economic Forum (WEF), the Bank for International Settlements (BIS) and of course, the World Bank, as well. Countries like China have happily borrowed trillions of dollars to get into the global space of Special Drawing Rights (SDR) of the IMF gaining every privilege to play in the global field. Even the U.S. has witnessed a huge inflation and debts currently due to the war.

The U.S – China rift, sanctions on Russia, the unstoppable Covid-19 implications are just catalytic factors that add more rage to the already rampant cold war. The Chinese drones, Russian entry into crypto-currencies and nuke-weapons trade constitute billions of dollars – cause an unbalanced economy amongst the stakeholder nations. While a group of elites and economists working for normalizing the global economy to certain standards, there do exist a provocative business deals and inundating scheme of things transforming the whole economic scene. The plots and plans for politico-economic developments are becoming bizarre and complicated, transforming it into a boxing ring where the players punch each other to win, and causing more destruction than development.

The U.S.-China eclipsing on Russia-Ukraine war

Obviously, the U.S. is not behind this Russia-Ukraine war. It is just the timing of the invasion on Ukraine by Russia creates an implausible thought of America playing a shadow role in the war that is lasting more than a fortnight now. Ever since the spread of pandemic from Wuhan laboratories, China, America has never been comfortable as it was deflected to fight aggressively in eradicating Covid-19 virus, and finding cure and vaccines and more importantly, the new models and modus-operands in restoring resilience and usual life. Even before the waves of pandemic cease to come to a new normal, the invasion plan by the Russian President Vladimir Putin has raised shock waves in the U.S. and the entire world.

In this invasion attempt by Russia, China remains a close ally of Russia. Actually, it does not mean that China is Ukraine's enemy. Russia and China, being the stronghold Communist nations, they have been sharing values and political strategies for many years. While Russia was part of Soviet Union, China supported Ukraine and other parts of the union. The disbanding of the Soviet Union has made Ukraine a little liberal, sovereign country. Russia's aggressive nature and its tendency to control the other smaller nations along its borders are there for years although it is acceptable and beneficial to those nations. Ukraine is the only exception, which has its history of being an origin of Russian ethnicity that began with Kievan Rus' as cultural ancestors. The Ukrainian capital city of Kiev dominated the Slavic state of Kievan Rus as a medieval, political federation during 862-1242 C.E. The modern states of Belarus and Russia derived their names from this medieval state.

However, it is all not between Russia and Ukraine alone. If there is war in Ukraine, it does affect the rest of the world, more specifically the European Union. From there, it impinges on the rest of the world. The U.S. being a super cop of the world might not have chance to see this effect from a posture distant from the warring region, but expecting serious implications in global economy as pointed out by International Monetary Fund (IMF), International Atomic Energy Agency (IAEA) and other international bodies. We are not in the times when there is a fight between the two countries that the world would simply sit back and watch the war happening elsewhere. A war means a lot of economic damage and causes unimaginable threats.

When the U.S. called for a U.N. Security Council's resolution on holding Russia accountable for its invasion on Ukraine on 25th February, 2022, China, India and United Arab Emirates abstained from voting. Reacting to Russia vetoing the resolution, the U.S responded strongly when the U.S. Ambassador to the United Nations, Linda Thomas Greenfield saying, "You can veto this resolution, but you cannot veto your voices. You cannot veto the truth; you cannot veto the Ukrainian people…"

Another alarming decision from Putin about putting nuclear forces under alert has also made the U.S. to choose a kind and strategic posture rather inducing a provocation in the European Union and Ukraine. It seems that the U.S. has categorically made up its mind not to conflict with Russia. It also denied Russia's false supposition that it was under threat from the U.S. and North-Atlantic Treaty Organization (NATO) forces.

Through the services of the United Nations, the U.S. has all the plans for stopping Russia's aggression and facilitating the rehabilitation of Ukrainian refugees. By imposing heavy sanctions on Russia and making systemic changes in the global financial modules like SWIFT, the U.S. is very keen to give Russia a blow it deserves. Even technological constraints imposed in Russia's computer and mobile phone market making it harder for the Russians to communicate to the rest of the world. When the U.S. does these sanctions, others follow as well. Thus, almost completely isolated Russia would have to realize the true potential of harmonious approach towards its aspirations on Ukraine.

Amid all these shocking reactions from the U.S. and other nations, Ukraine's call to NATO for the announcement of 'no-fly-zone over the skies of Ukraine' was declined firmly as it would vouch for a direct fight between Russia and NATO. America with its influence in the European Union and NATO might have gone in support for Ukraine's plea but preferred not to interfere rather focusing on economic sanctions and banning of crude oil from Russia. Combating Russia directly from the U.S. end would explicitly display the true character of America and animosity with its age-old rival and its new opponent China.

Even while America is fuming over the pandemic allegedly caused by China, it strongly imposed ban on Chinese Apps, electronic products and cut-short its ties with the Asian country. Literally, America was waiting for a strategic space for countering China's mischievous Covid dart that hit upon every aspects of life in the world.

Russia-Ukraine war too has shadows of similar kind of reactions from the world since no other country could directly indulge into the matters of these two warring nations. The U.S. just concluded its operations in Afghanistan have no say on this, as well. Yet, it is trying to see a diplomatic end to the war as that would bring gains in securing more control over Russia directly in the global arena. Indirectly, it has also passed a fitting message to China over its past mistakes. And, that puts America in to a kind of shadow diplomacy at this juncture of Russia-Ukraine war

The Third World War

Among the top ten importers of major arms in the world during the decade that spans 2011-2021, India, Saudi Arabia and Egypt stand at the first three rankings in this charter. Among the top ten exporters in the world during the same decade, America, Russia and France stand at the first three rankings. Arms and weapons deal has been a great business amongst the developed countries and the developing countries as well due to the fact that the need for defence, security and power play has been steadily growing in last few decades. Economic development and subsequent emerging competition to stay economically fit has made many countried to grow their stock in terms of arms and weapons. Bigger nations continue to rein over this market of warheads as they continue to export more missiles and warheads to the smaller, developing nations.

Just as progress been made in other sectors like oil, energy, gold, electronics, machinery and automobiles, weapons trade has also been widening over the years. While other markets are targeting the consumers at large, weapons do have a remarkable need for a nation to add strength to its power and defencive strategies. In the on going war between Russia and Ukraine, it has come to light that the conventional idea of this weapons trade and related might behind nations has been countermanded since nations, especially those belonging to NATO, extend their support to Ukraine by supplying more arms and weapons.

The Arms Trade Treaty(ATT), regulating the international trade in conventional arms that include small arms to battle tanks, combat aircraft and warships is in effect since 24 December 2014. More than half of the nations in the world have not signed and joined this treaty proposed by the United Nations. The ATT establishes common standards for the international trade of weapons and seeks to reduce the illicit arms trade.

When it comes to war, all such treaties are violated. Even deadly weapons are being traded to the nation under seige during war. The very need for ATT seeing to promote justice, peace and security has been defeated as the nations cite the same factors for aiding with arms and weapons during the war. In the current Russia-Ukraine war, NATO countries feel that the invasion by Russia as unjustifiable, devastative military action, and decided to supply Ukraine with arms and weapons. If Russia uses nuclear arms, NATO might also aid Ukraine with its nuclear arsenal. One of the main reasons for such a development is that Ukraine is giving a tough fight on Russia's attacks by counter-attacks. Secondly, NATO counties do not directly deal with Russia rather preferred to help Ukraine in its warring strategies. Whatever, supplying of arms and weapons to aggravate the war on Ukraine is haplessly fuelling Russia to continue its war.

The United Nations and peace promoting agencies in the world must have to condemn this action by NATO to stop the war and promote global peace. And, this could be the first step towards impeding the possible Third World War.

Hopes and Premonitions

Will civil unrest break out? Will there be a democratic revolution? Will there be peace with the emergence of a new president and government? Will the military take over the regime and continue to fight with Russia?

Even a minor drone strike by Ukraine provokes Russia. The thought of nuclear war is only due to Ukraine attacks on and near Moscow.

NATO countries have not yet stopped sending weapons and equipment to Ukraine. Ukraine cannot become a

NATO member unless the war stops. This is not a bilateral issue like the India-Pakistan war on PoK. It is yet to be ascertained to find if the ongoing war limited itself to both countries. It requires stringent decisions from NATO, Russia and Ukraine from their individual perspectives!

The Great World War I lasted for four years and the Second World War for six years. With the current mind-set of Russia, especially after the killing of the chief of the Wagner group in a plane crash, the war seemed to focus on the war and only war, no other options. Ukraine also is not budging nor does it go all out to pull NATO countries directly indulging into a large-scale war.

Ukraine is already under siege because of retaliatory attacks. If not stopped, the war will escalate. His call for holding elections in 2024 will not happen. In Russia, Putin is still a favourite candidate for next year's presidential election.

The unending attacks between Russia and Ukraine send frightening signals to the rest of the world, as well. However, NATO countries do not seem to fear war of any kind. It seems that the war will expand and the fear of war will engulf other Soviet countries as well.

The people of Ukraine have nothing to do in the interim. It is now imperative to find a better way to change the president and change the ruling power. Peaceful negotiations with Russia and the postponement of NATO membership will only happen if the Ukrainian people stage a revolution. Only then is it possible for Ukrainians who have fled could return to their country.

What will be the future of Ukraine and Russia? The never-ending war and attacks seem to end only if a nuclear attack would give a big jolt on either of the countries. The war that began with tanks and missile attacks has now been reduced to drone attacks and a massive civilian clash is not a surprise in the near future. Ukraine would return to peace only if it aligned with NATO in its fullest devotion, which requires a peace accord with Russia.

Climate Change: Issues and Actions

Climate Change has been a serious threat in many parts of the world, these days. As the U.N. categorically warned that the world is heading on a highway towards a climate hell, we do know that the world governments are already taking steps in addressing the climate change issues. Brazil, America, Australia, Germany, Netherlands have begun their part early 2022 in clearing up the mess that was destructing the climate in their countries.

Until a decade ago, climate change activists were not serious enough to address the issue or to say it bluntly, could not put it in the right perspective. Global warming was the only slogan spoken across the globe indicating that the earth the very planet we live upon, is heating up. Icebergs melt, oceans reduce in some continents like Asia whereas it grows in some other continents like North America increasing sea level, wild fires causing huge destruction to natural vegetation – are just a few abnormalities what the world was witnessing. Adding to this were calamities like volcanoes spitting ash and lava, earthquakes, twisters and hurricanes, cloud bursts causing incessant rains and flooding of reservoirs with dangerous levels of storage and landslides changing the entire landscape etc. Having experienced these natural catastrophes, people still were 'climate change deniers'. There was lack of political will and a big question of acceptance of 'climate change' as an issue, at all, to speak about in public forums, conferences and meetings. It was dubbed later as an intellectual ignorance from the part of people who deny all about climate is an outcome human interferences on this planet. David Slesinger of the U.S.A, one of the pioneers of all climate change activists of all-time said, *"Just as they are comfortably ignorant about evidence of human-made climate change, we are comfortable with our ignorance of Gandhi's approach to nonviolent resistance,"* while referring to the climate-change deniers and those who did not want to realize that it was a serious issue.

Green campaigns began only to flourish after the year 2010. People started to work towards pollution-free, cleaner world. Movements for cleaner air, water, land have come into action with slogans for conserving natural resources for a sustainable living. Environmental cleanliness was given more importance than ever before. Farmers, Fishermen and flight operators began to realize the effects of climate change, and are most severely affected as they witnessed unpredictable rainfalls, undue drought conditions, frequent cyclones and randomness (either delayed or early) in changing seasons. By 2013, climate change, environment and sustainable development have become a main topic of learning and research in many universities across the world.

During the course of studying climate change, many definitions and perceptions about it have also cropped up. While some see it as a change in global or regional climate patterns causing atmospheric disorders, others observe it as a change in the constituents of natural resources like air, water and land. Researchers found it as a change in geographical patterns causing disturbing conditions making it harder for inhabiting a particular place or the planet as a whole.

Today, climate change talks have come in plenty and climate action has emerged as a direct question on the face of drastic rise in the sea levels, loss of biodiversity and ecosystem, intense heat waves and drought conditions. Atmospheric pollution caused due to the extreme use of fossil fuels, spread of highly infectious diseases, greenhouse effect add more damage to the normal conditions in the ecosystem required for all life including human beings. Increasing population, global warming, changing climatic conditions, felling of trees, silted water bodies, environmental degradation, all these add up to the problem of depletion of water resources.

The First World Climate Conference was held on 12–23 February 1979 in Geneva principally focusing on global warming, and climate research and forecasting. The first UN Climate Change Conference was held in 1995 in Berlin. Today's agenda of the meetings under the banner of climate change has turned into a new sphere of global factors and standards. Fossil fuel vehicles contribute 80% to the carbon levels in atmosphere.

During the civil war in 2007, Sudan witnessed unprecedented scarce of water due to changing rainfall patterns. UN Secretary General Ban Ki-moon described the conflict in Sudan's Darfur region as the world's first climate change conflict. Dr. Vesselin Popovski, the Head of the United Nations University Institute of Sustainability and Peace's Peace and Security Section argues that there is an indirect link between climate change and conflict. According to him, the causes of conflict are first political and economic, not climatic. Warlords, who foster conflict, may exploit draught, flooding, starvation, agricultural or natural disasters in their strategies, like they did in Somalia and Darfur. But what will drive their fight is not the rain, the temperature, or the sea level, they will always fight for the same goals of power, territory, money, revenge, etc.

People depend, respond and adapt to changes in natural resources and ecosystems. The most vulnerable landscapes falling into the grip of drought conditions in Sudan is the best example for climate change affecting the inhabitants! The changing conditions change the lives of the people over there.

Adding to the climate change, disasters cause environmental hazards that interact with physical, social, and economic vulnerabilities reflecting harmful human impacts such as lost lives and livelihoods, and displacement.

The effects of climate change have increasingly become a direct challenge to smaller, developing island nations. In 2014, islets of the Central-Pacific Polynesian island of Kiribati were submerged due to rise in sea level forcing the inhabitants to flee for resettlement and rehabilitation. Climate change perpetuates violence and conflict, intensifies poverty and fragility of the state as the affected people know no ways to adapt to the changing conditions and damaged environment. Various clashes between pastorals and farmers in Northern Nigeria seemed to be an outcome of environmental stress. In Pakistan's water scarcity is creating provincial conflicts and big political divides. Heavy floods in 2010 and 2011 have flown into sea gratuitously that could otherwise have catered to the needs of people for atleast 10 to 15 years. No political consensus was reached for constructing the dam for storing excess water. This conflict created food scarcity, water-sharing conflicts and power shortages.

A 2014 report by the UN University, Institute for Environment and Human Security (UNU-EHS) and the Norwegian Refugee Council (NRC) says that drought forced people to leave their homes in Somalia and Ethiopia and fled to Kenya, Egypt or Yemen. Most of those fleeing were pastoralists, small scale farmers and agro-pastoralists.

Lessons learned:

"Peace, development and environmental protection are interdependent and indivisible."

"There is a link between climate change and conflict, migration"

COP27 held at Egypt in 2022 give us a new insight on dealing with climatic changes and effects across the globe. The stakeholder countries are tirelessly facilitating the plans and schemes suggested at the climate meets held in various parts of the world. To reduce carbon emission and global warming, many countries have unveiled policies and measures that could cut carbon emissions through automobiles, thermal plants and other industries that pollute air, water, and landscapes. Electric vehicles replacing fossil fuel based automobiles, electronic transactions to reduce the use of paper and deforestation, renewable energy to replace thermal and nuclear plants, renewed waste management techniques – all these have become priorities in many parts of the world.

In 2015, India unveiled its official climate action goals. Implementing policies like odd-even-number rules to reduce traffic congestion, disposing of diesel-based vehicles, subsidies for consuming solar energy, refurbished rainwater harvesting, and water management techniques for combating greenhouse effect – all these are in place. India set the 100GW solar energy target by the year 2026 of which 70% has been achieved. While major global forces are expecting a complete overhauling of the system in developing countries, changing the frivolous climatic conditions to the global standards is not only a challenging task but also a critical task in the face of recessive economic conditions and inflation.

Renewable energy manufacturing is one sector what the world intends to focus on to develop a sustainable climate action. The U.N. has its goal of reducing the impacts of climate change by half by 2030 and reach net-zero by 2050. Bioenergy, geothermal, hydropower, ocean, solar and wind energy – all these seem to be climate imperative to cut down greenhouse gas emissions.

At the time of fluctuating economic conditions and unstoppable inflation of prices, bringing a 'new normal' to meet the effects of climate changes is really frightening step for any nation to proceed further. Costs incurring to tackle abnormal climate changes is high and infeasible sometimes.

Therefore, the current measures do not suffice enough to answer all of the threats posed by the nature. We need to revise ourselves where we started and what needs to be done! What climate change actions are taken concretely to tackle the issue? - And, to what improvement is achieved by those actions? Even as the whole world is working towards much greener, cooler planet Earth, every one of us never fail to ask at what cost the climate change actions are implemented year after year?

Predictions unveiled at COP27 about savings are unbelievably exciting. Pledges and assurances are also in plenty: Savings up to $410 billion in energy efficiency initiatives; Reassurance of $100 billion a year in aid funding pledged in 2015 Paris climate agreement, etc..., etc... Green transition that includes creating energy-efficient infrastructures, manufacturing e-vehicles will provide more than 24 million jobs by 2030, the U.N. reports.

Setting aside the criticism over the climate change actions suggested by the world environmental organizations headed by rich nations, there arises a definite question about where the money would come from to meet the costs of these new projects and policies. It is high time now to check the results obtained from the climate change actions carried out until this point. When the existing industries causing environmental and climatic damages are facing a closure, nation's economy suffers; employment suffers. On top of that finding alternative industries means extra burden on investments and costs! So, both criticism and fiscal deficit dissuade new climate action plans. Why because the world cannot afford a new liability to create new assets!

Remember the phrase, "One stride forward, and two steps backward". Right now, this is the situation when it comes to climate Change Action! With thousands of tonnes of pollutants in air and water, we have just few hundred billion dollars to work on it. As global temperature is rising by 1.5% every year, we just have to stop exhausting natural resources, and burning fossil fuels. Nothing more. Nothing less.

Index

References

- *Taking Sarvodaya to the People*, R. R. Keithahn
- *India of my Dreams*, M.K. Gandhi
- *Vinoba-Sahitya, Vol. 16* (Paramdham Prakashan, Pavnar, 1996), p. 285.
- *Arthasastra, Book-I, Chapter VII.* Kautilya,
- *Constructive Programme,* M.K. Gandhi Chapter XIII
- *Unto this Last,* John Ruskin, p. 20, p.36
- *Gandhian economic thought*, J.C. Kumarappa, Chapter V, p.49
- *Young India*, 4-12-1924, p. 398
- *Harijan*, 27-5-1939, p. 143
- *Gandhi's Epigram,* mkgandhi.org
- *Reflections of Gandhi*, George Orwell
- *Cooperative Commonwealth* by Surendra Bhana
- *Gandhiji's letter to Mr. M.A. Jinnah*, 24 September 1944
- *Jinnah Gandhi talks 1944*, Cabinet Mission Plan
- *Wikipedia/Conflict Management*
- *Wikipedia/Conflict Resolution*
- *Wikipedia/U.S-Iran relations*
- *Wikipedia/U.S-North Korea relations*
- *Conflict Resolution: Glimpses from Gandhi's public life, Balamurali Balaji*
- *The Hindu, dated 25th June 2019*
- *Harijan, 29 Aug 1936, p. 226*
- *Mahatma Gandhi: The Last Phase, Vol X, Pyarelal Nayyar, p.552*
- *Harijan, 27 Feb 1937, p.18*
- *Harijan, 4 Nov 1939, p. 331*
- *Young India, 13 Oct. 1921,*
- *Young India, 27 Oct. 1921,*
- *Young India, 26 Dec. 1924*
- *Harijan, 31 Mar 1946, p.63*

- *Harijan, 25 Oct 1952*
- *Hind Swaraj and Other Writings, Anthony J. Parel, Cambridge: Cambridge University Press, 1997, p.81.*
- *Hind swaraj*
- *Young India, July 17, 1924*
- *Contextualising Gandhian thought, Siby K. Joseph, Institute of Gandhian Studies, Wardha*
- *Young India, Dec 26, 1924.*
- *From Yeravda Mandir, M. K. Gandhi,. Navajivan Press, Ahmedabad, 2nd edition, 1935.*
- *Harijan, July 20, 1947*
- *Substantiating the TGP through Vinoba's Philosophy, Article by Balamurali Balaji, p 2*
- *Harijan, 2-1-1937, p. 374*
- *Anasakti Darshan, July 2010-June 2011*
- *Mahatma Gandhi's Ideas: C.F. Andrews; George Allen, London, 1929.*
- *The Mind of Mahatma Gandhi, R. K. Prabhu & U. R. Rao*
- *Harijan, 25-3-1939, p. 64*
- *Selections from Gandhi, Nirmal Kumar Bose, Navajivan Mudranalaya, Ahmedabad*
- *Harijan, 29-8-1936, p. 226*
- *Young India, 10-2-1927, p. 44*
- *Wikipedia/Islamic Terror*
- *Harijan, 27 Feb 1937, p.18*
- *Pyarelal Nayyar, Mahatma Gandhi: The Last Phase, Vol X, p.552*
- *J. C. Kumarappa, Gandhian Economic Thought, p.3*
- *Dr. Vishwanath Tandon, Is Gandhi out of date, p.32*

- *Dr.A.S. Sasikala, Environmental thoughts of Gandhi for a green future, Gandhi Marg, Volume 34*
- *Balamurali Balaji, 'The Techno-Gandhian Philosophy', CIT-GPNP*
- *'National Green Tribunal', Times of India, 23rd July, 2020*
- *'Draft EIA notification', The Indian Express, 11th August, 2020*
- *http://blog.ipleaders.in/ngt-judgments/amp/*
- *https://en.m.wikipedia.org/wiki/Market_Economy*
- *https://www.brittanica.com/topic/economic-development*
- *https://www.downtoearth.org.in/blog/environment/amp/environmental-impact-assessment*
- *The Techno-Gandhian News, Monthly Journal May 2020 - June 2021,*
- *The pandemic as a catalyst for remote work culture*
- *https://observatory.tec.mx/edu-news/pandemic-catalyst-for-remote-work*
- *https://www.nytimes.com/2020/05/05/business/pandemic-work-from-home-coronavirus.html*
- *Harijan, 6-5-1939, p113, M. K. Gandhi, Navajivan Publishing House, Ahmadabad*
- *The Techno-Gandhian News, Monthly Journal May 2020, June 2020*
- *https://observatory.tec.mx/edu-news/pandemic-catalyst-for-remote-work*
- *https://www.nytimes.com/2020/05/05/business/pandemic-work-from-home-coronavirus.html*
- *Harijan, 6-5-1939, p113,*